THE ART OF BRAND STORYTELLING

MUSA ADI

Copyright © 2021 Musa Adi
All rights reserved.
ISBN: **9798540993029**

DEDICATION

I gratefully dedicate this book to my daughter Jood.
Also, to, my mother, you will always be the reason for me to stay strong.

ACKNOWLEDGMENTS

"I have to thank Almighty Allah for my faith in him did not allow me fading despite what happened to me when I lost everything. I never imagined myself as a writer or author, but my destiny has other plans for me that I truly never imagined. I found myself again and decided that I will never allow myself to fall again and here I am starting this journey. I will not stop at this book, and I will continue my writing journey exploring more ideas, topics and getting deeply into more emotional adventures."

Foreword

In today's marketplace, marketers are facing a big dilemma in delivering brand messages to consumers due to the huge number of ads that are all over the place. The big question that many ask is "How to hook a customer and penetrate through the noisy distracted markets?

Many people think that branding is just a logo, colors, and a tagline. However, a brand is not just a visual identity or a product or what is written in a mission statement. This book is about brand storytelling that builds an emotional connection with the audience because simply human brains are shaped to respond to stories. Brand Storytelling is not about what brands sell but they are stories that clarify what brands do for their customers in solving their problems and provide better-personalized user experiences that make consumers more comfortable and satisfied. Marketers shall utilize the power of storytelling in making the audience and the consumers part of the brand's story. The earliest humans gathered around the campfire and believed that effective storytelling was the best way to communicate the information that was vital for survival. Humans figured out that connecting with their communities in an emotional manner was a matter of life and death. Storytelling is not just entertainment; it is an emotional and identification journey. It gives a sense of purpose, identity, and continuity between the past and the present. It is doing more than just conveying a message; the story is a container for deepest longings, hopes, and fears and forces self-reflection and articulation.

About the Author

Musa is an entrepreneur and a senior business leader who worked in various managerial positions with over 17 years of experience specializing in management and compliance, marketing, business risk management, project management, operational risk, and enterprise infrastructure and operations for clients in the oil & gas, manufacturing, engineering, and food industries. Musa holds a master's degree in International Management from the University of Liverpool and a certificate in cybersecurity management from the University of Toronto, a diploma in Project Management, and a BSc degree in electrical power engineering technology.

Table of Contents

Chapter 1		11
1.1	What Is Brand Storytelling	11
1.2	What Is Personalization	12
1.3	Storytelling Triangular Pillars	14
1.4	References	18
Chapter 2		19
2.1	Why Do We Need Storytelling?	19
2.2	References	27
Chapter 3		29
3.1	The Elements Of A Story	29
3.2	Story Brand Purpose And Goal	30
3.3	References	31
Chapter 4		32
4.1	The Conflict	32
4.2	The Opposite Counterparts	33
4.3	Adversaries	35
4.4	Struggles	36
4.1	References	36
Chapter 5		37
5.1	Hero	37
5.2	The Hero Journey	40
5.3	References	41
Chapter 6		42
6.1	The Plot	42

6.2	Robin Hood And Cause Marketing Plot Template	44
6.3	Sustainability Plot Template	48
6.4	References	49

Chapter 7 50

7.1	The Villain	50
7.2	Southwest Airlines "Transfarency"	51
7.3	References	52

Chapter 8 53

8.1	A Purpose Corporate Core Message Story	53
8.2	Believe In Something Everything	54
8.3	Forever Against Animal Testing: Join The Fight!	55
8.4	"Sustainability Is Now As Important As Safety To Us"	56
8.5	Bosch Revolves Around The "Invented For Life"	59
8.6	Doing It Right At First Time With Constant Care	60
8.7	United Breaks The Guitar	62
8.8	References	65

Chapter 9 67

9.1	Difference Between Case Studies And Stories	67
9.2	Dove Real Beauty Sketches	69
9.3	References	71

Chapter 10 73

10.1	Apply The Story Model	73
10.2	Brand Storytelling Model	73
10.3	Storytelling Concepts For A Brand	78
10.4	References	80

Chapter 11 81

11.1	A Corporate Core Story Vs. Brand Story	81
11.2	Brand Story	83
11.3	Holistic Approach Storytelling..	84
11.4	3m's 15% Culture Of Innovation And Sustainability	85
11.5	References	86

Chapter 12 87

12.1	The Significant Role Of Ceos In The Brand Storytelling......	87
12.2	References	91

Chapter 13 92

13.1	Gaps In Storytelling	92
13.2	Warby Parker Brand's Personality...................................	94
13.3	References	96

Chapter 14 97

14.1	Storytelling In Advertising...	97
14.2	Travelers Real-Life Story Ads "Unfinished Story"	98
14.3	Nescafé Gold Blend Love Story......................................	99
14.4	Discover Your Wings – University Of Phoenix	101
14.5	References	102

Chapter 15 103

Storytelling Is A Powerful Communication Tool 103

15.1	Brand Communication	103
15.2	Brand Authentic And Communication Messages	110
15.3	The Purpose Law	111
15.4	Communicating The Purpose And Culture	112

15.5	Brand Communication In Social Media	117
15.6	Brand Communication Through Logos And Colors	125
15.7	References	128

Chapter 16 130

16.1	What Is A Visual Story?	130
16.2	The Power Of Brand Visualization	130
16.3	Social Media Role In Brand Storytelling	132
16.4	References	143

Chapter 1

1.1 WHAT IS BRAND STORYTELLING

Brand Storytelling is a narrative to communicate a message to the potential customers and existing consumers. Human brains are rooted to respond to stories thanks to their psychological nature. The brand storytelling goal is to tempt the customers' desire and inspire them to connect with a brand to make an action, to buy a product or service. Brand Storytelling helps customers understand why they should care about a brand, product, individual, or company. A personalized story allows the brand to change customers' lives because it solves their problems and it customizes its products or services to fulfill customer demands, wishes, and dreams and provide a better user experience. For example, Apple recently released robust new privacy protections in the iOS operating system which help users better control and manage access to their data. These features represent the latest innovations in Apple's legacy of privacy leadership. [1]

Why is privacy so important to apple? And how can this be linked to personalized customer user experience in brand storytelling? According to apple, privacy is a fundamental human right. It is also one of its core values. Customers' devices are essential to many parts of people's life. What users share from those experiences and whom they share it with should be up to them. Apple designs products to protect users' privacy and give them control over their information. In Apple's personalized privacy story, the company decided to fight against adversaries who were using IOS operating systems to track users over the internet and influence their purchasing behaviors by bombarded tailored ads and artificial intelligence advanced technology without users' knowledge and approval.

1.2 WHAT IS PERSONALIZATION

In 2012 New York Times article called, "How Companies Learn Your Secrets." It was written mainly as a follow-up to what became a public incident: An angry father marched into a Minnesota Target store, demanded to know why his teenage daughter received coupons for baby products, only to find out later that she was pregnant. The retailer could predict her pregnancy and subsequently personalize the promotions she received, thanks to a ton of -completely legal- data collection and analysis.[2] Some may argue that this is not ethical, whereas others see it as just ok. The bottom line is that personalization aims to help consumers and make them more comfortable not to invade their privacy.

Personalized stories keep context more relevant and meaningful for life, work, relationships, and community norms. It grabs customers' attention because it is easier to consume and engage, makes them think, and inspires them to act. Harvard Business School professor Gerald Zaltman said that 95% of purchase decision-making occurs in consumers' subconscious minds.[3]

Personalization drives engagement and builds relationships. Personalization offers customers tailored experiences that keep them engaged and is essential to remaining competitive in a crowded and increasingly savvy marketplace. As a result, customers today are gravitating toward brands that feel like they listen to them, understand them, and pay attention to their specific wants and needs. According to each customer's unique profile, it is a way for brands to contextualize the messages, offers, and experiences they deliver. The digital age has leveraged consumer expectations for relevant, contextual, and convenient experiences to extraordinary levels. Consumers have become habituated to getting what they want, and they are leaning toward the brands that recognize them as individuals at every step of their journey.

According to an (Accenture 2018) survey, 91% of consumers are more likely to shop with brands that recognize, remember, and provide them with relevant offers and recommendations.[4] Emotions are personal to humans, and that personal connection is something that savvy brands are leveraging via contextual marketing. In contrast, non-personalization is like a one-size-fits-all that has no consideration for customer preferences. Preference for personalized experiences helps customers to reduce their overload consumption for information. Further, it allows brands to tailor their products, ads, offers, services to suit consumer's preferences. If brands want to break through the to reach their consumers and keep them emotionally connected clutter, they shall infuse personalization into their storytelling. The role of storytelling is to support the brands.

No one does personalization quite like streaming giant Netflix, and it all comes down to being entirely data-driven. It is an approach that is paying off as Netflix is now the top choice for video streaming in all the global regions. It has become a well-known fact that no two Netflix homepages look the same, owing to the tracking and algorithms used by the service. "Netflix is streaming in over 30 languages and 190 countries because marvelous stories can come from anywhere and be loved everywhere". [5]

Storytelling is not limited to films; stories can be told in pictures, verbally or written, or exposed across all channels, from social media to billboards. As a result, stories can help marketers achieve cut-through and reduce their ad expenditures in a noisy, distracting marketplace and create advertising that resonates with people and sticks with them. A successful story is a dynamic escalation of conflict-driven events that cause meaningful change in the main character's life. Storytelling is not just entertainment; it is an emotional and identification journey. It gives a sense of purpose, identity, and continuity between the past and the present. It is doing more than just conveying a message; the story is a container for deepest longings, hopes, and fears—storytelling forces self-reflection.

1.3 STORYTELLING TRIANGULAR PILLARS

Storytelling involves a three-way relationship involving the storyteller, the story, and the audience, who is in our narrative is the customer. Storytelling is about connections, sharing values and emotions with consumers. It is not to dictate conclusions to the consumers. It helps the consumers see inside a situation—the world of the story—and the insider of the characters' feelings and struggles. Storytelling includes characters, setting, conflict, rising action, climax, and denouement, finally resolving a happy ending.

A GOOD STORY IS WHAT REALLY WORKS

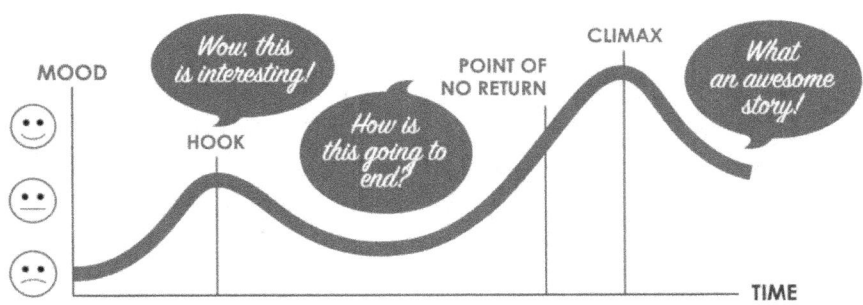

Figure 1-1 Story Journey

Creating these pillars allows consumers to follow a story easily—and remember it. The main character in storytelling is not a brand or company; it is the customer. The customer must be the hero or a victim, while the brand is the guide during the journey. Assume a brand wants to be a hero in its ad story. In that case, it must tell the audience a story about its entrepreneurial journey from rags to rich in inspiring others who face similar struggles and conflicts and want to succeed not to quit till they reach their desired goals.

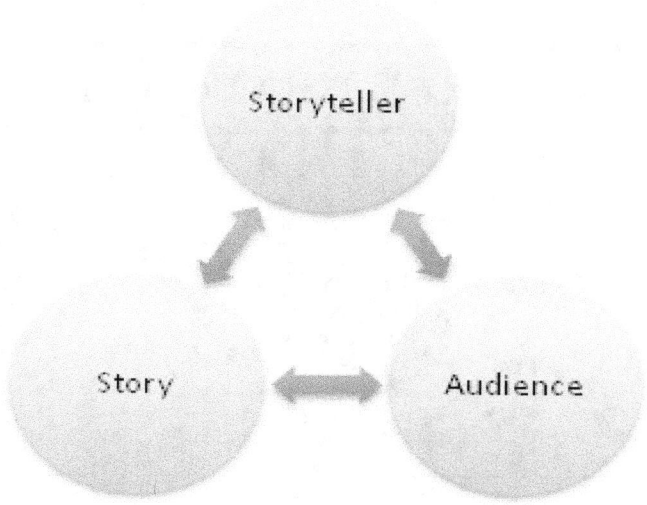

Figure 1-2 Storytelling involves a three-way relationship

"Purpose" is about values – values about who brands are, what they stand for, what they do for others, and the causes they serve. An obvious purpose gives consumers a way to connect with a brand and its values and products or services that add real value to people's lives beyond just selling things to making profits. For example, Nike stands for "Bring inspiration and innovation to every athlete in the world," not for sports equipment.[6] Disney stands for family happiness, not theme parks or movies. Brands that can successfully target consumers based on these shared values are the ones who will ultimately win their attention and purchasing power. That is why big brands like Nike, Coca-Cola, Pepsi, Unilever, and Adidas are turning to purpose to better connect and engage with their consumers. But, of course, purpose cannot be activated and reinforced without storytelling.

As a marketer, you need to connect customers with brand values, drive them to the brand's purpose, and communicate that story to the audience. This type of narrative is necessary for consumers to accept the brand message and be inspired to join the brand's purpose and tribe.

A splendid story must be authentic and genuine. Finding that story may require a profound reflection on values and sharing personal experiences and moments with consumers.

The three influential ways storytellers end a story is by allowing the hero to

1. Winsome sort of power or position

2. Be unified with somebody or something

3. Experience a self-fulfillment

These are the three most employed story endings because they are dominant psychological desires shared by most human beings.

A well-told story captures people's attention, holds them in suspense, and pays off with a meaningful emotional experience. Emotional because people sympathize with the story characters; meaningful because the hero's actions deliver internal insights into human nature. [7]

1.4 REFERENCES

1. Apple (2021) *Apple advances its privacy leadership with iOS 15, iPadOS 15, macOS Monterey, and watchOS 8* https://apple.co/2TBws1A
2. Duhigg, C. (2012, Feb.16) *How companies learn your secrets* https://nyti.ms/2UrVHDn
3. Mahoney, M (2003, Jan 13) *The subconscious mind of the consumer (And how to reach it),* https://hbs.me/2TwivlE
4. Accenture (2018) *Widening gap between consumer expectations and reality in personalization signals Warning for brands, accenture interactive research finds,* https://accntu.re/3wiAyce
5. Netflix (2021) About netflix, https://about.netflix.com/en
6. Nike (2021) For once, Don't Do It | Nike, https://purpose.nike.com/what-we-stand-for
7. Miller, D. (2017) *Building a StoryBrand: Clarify Your Message So Customers Will Listen,* HarperCollins Leadership, pp. 96, https://amzn.to/2RLERhU

Chapter 2

2.1 WHY DO WE NEED STORYTELLING?

In his book permission marketing (1999), Seth Godin wrote we are exposed to one million commercial messages that in one year, 3000 messages every day! 1 (Yankelovich 2007), a market research firm, estimated that a person living in a city 30 years ago watched up to 2,000 ad messages a day, compared with up to 5,000 per day at the time of the research in 2007. About half the 4,110 people surveyed by Yankelovich said they thought marketing and advertising were out of control.2 This was before social media grown and heavily influenced people's habits and lifestyles. Nowadays, consumers are much more exposed to advertising and marketing messages as people spend more time on the internet. (Statista 2020) reported that internet users' average daily social media usage accounted for 145 minutes per day in 2020, up from 142 minutes in 2019. 3 Ad spending in the social media advertising segment is projected to reach US$110,628m in 2021. 4 Americans checked their smartphones once every 10 minutes 96 times a day, according to recent research by a global tech care company (Asurion 2019). 5 Unless ad campaigns are attractive and clear in its' purpose and call to action, consumers will skip & ignore them. In partnership with Nielsen, AOL released a research study in 2011 that revealed 27 million pieces of online content are shared daily in the U.S. alone. Results also showed that 53% of time spent on the Internet was directly attributable to content consumption. 6

How many marketing messages get stored in an average consumer's memory, considering they probably could not care less about advertising and sales talk? One or two? Three, if we are optimistic? Three out of several thousand! If this is even halfway true, there must be many companies out there who waste an awful lot of money on ineffective marketing. Storytelling lets marketers "get inside the heads" of a prospect's customer. It creates emotions, paint pictures, and channel the desires, hopes, and dreams of a customer. Stories are the best ways to capture customer attention (and hold it), and by nature, they are highly shareable — people like to repeat stories and pass them around because they remember them. To retain customers' loyalty in today's aggressive competitive environment, marketers must create a personalized, relevant experience and differentiate a brand from rivals.

The physical product itself no longer has influences that drive the bond between a brand and the consumer. Human beings actively seek stories and experiences in pursuit of a meaningful life. Similarly, companies need to communicate their messages based on values and clearly illustrate how they make a difference for ordinary customers seeking solutions to their problems. Companies need to rethink how to influence and build emotional connections with their audience and their employees. Storytelling and purpose branding can make widely impact on consumers if they join together. A strong brand builds on emotional values. They have clearly defined values, while a good story communicates those values in a language easily understood by the audience. Strong brand storytelling exists based on its emotional ties with the consumer; therefore, storytelling has the power to strengthen a brand both internally and externally. The stories are circulating in and around the company paint a picture of the company's culture and values, heroes and enemies, good points, and bad. By sharing these stories, brands define "who They are" and "What they stand for." As a result, many companies started to open their eyes to consumers' needs for an emotional dimension in branding.

The story behind the brand builds upon its values and culture, delivers both emotions and values, eventually helps to build a bridge between the company and the consumer- communicating more than mere price advantage. When companies and brands communicate and connect through stories, they help the customer shape his way in today's world. A well-perceived solid brand is the added value that a company or product represents, and it is a combination of realities and emotions. [7]

The memory of powerful emotional images and events may be at the expense of other information. Consequently, it is less likely to remember information followed by something intensely emotional. This effect appears to be more vital for women. An investigation of autobiographical memories found that positive memories contained more sensory and contextual details than neutral or negative memories. [8]

- Emotionally charged events are better remembered.
- Unpleasant emotions are less remembered than pleasant emotions ones.
- Positive memories contain more contextual details (which in turn, helps memory)
- Emotional excitement, not the importance of the information helps memory, and here comes the role

of emotional branding techniques.

(Nielsen 2017) studied brand memorability decay over a more extended period for several digital video ads. While recall dropped for all ads by 50% in the first 24 hours, it still stood at that same 50% level five days later for half of the brands. Nielsen concluded from its research that memories could persist either via repetition for specific types of memories or via implicit internalization. Emotional brand storytelling help consumers recognize and recall brand messages as their memory decay will last longer. 9

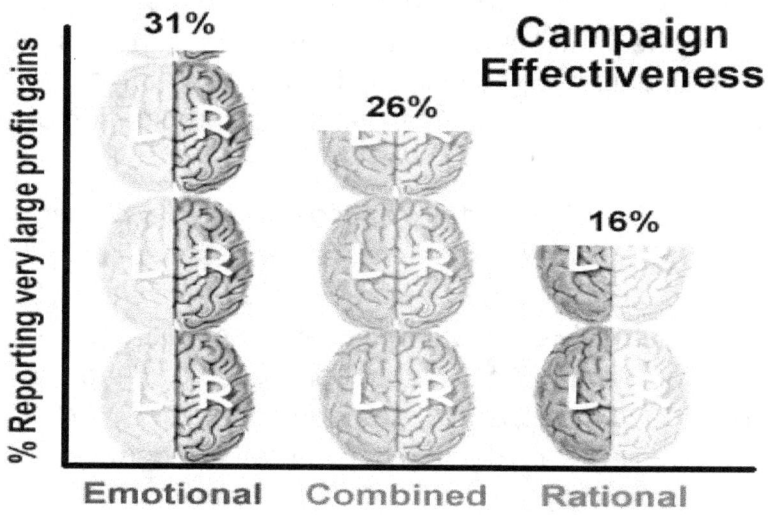

Figure 2-1 Emotional Ads Work Best

An analysis of data from the IPA (the U.K.-based Institute of Practitioners in Advertising) reveals that Ads campaigns with purely emotional content performed better (31% vs. 16%), about double comparing with only rational content. Ads with purely emotional make a slightly better (31% vs. 26%) than combined emotional and rational content.10 Committing to the emotive branding approach requires a deep understanding of consumer motivation. Nike's pervasive theme of "success in sport" is a case of a brand that centers its ads on a critical emotional driver and builds advertising, sponsorships around it. 11

Subaru's ads communicate "love" through a series of ads https://bit.ly/3alHKqg that puts the Autocar brand as a symbol of caring for those you love. Whether it is a father caring for his son or daughter, or a parent caring for their beloved pet, the series of ads are more about what the brand represents to the family by communicating the brand through stories, Subaru elevates its brand values and crystalizes how it fits into customers' lives.12

Figure 2-2 All-New 2021 Subaru Outback | Subaru Australia

In an (Accenture 2017) study on hyper-relevant customer experiences, 44% % are frustrated when companies fail to deliver relevant and personalized shopping experiences, 41% of consumers switched companies because of poor personalization, costing companies an estimated $756 billion in just one year. 13

According to a survey by (Infosys 2014), 86% of consumers say that personalization has some impact on what they purchase; and 25% admit personalization 'significantly influences' their buying decisions. 89% of shoppers who engage with retailers via social media channels say those interactions impacted their purchasing choices. 90% of retailers believed consistency across their brand's engagement points affected customer loyalty. These consumer surveys confirm the need for brand storytelling to engage and to connect with them. Failing to do so will waste many opportunities and marketing resources. 14

Chocolates and personalization best fit together, and Cadbury knew how to use them in its favor. The confectionery giant has found success with many personalization campaigns, raising brand awareness, increasing market penetration in unexplored territories, and building emotional connections with customers. In 2017 the chocolate brand used Personalized Video as a Service (PVaaS) to spread the word about its special Cadbury Glow gift chocolate in India https://bit.ly/3cDODKc. In this region, chocolate as gift-giving is less common than in other nations. So, the integrated social video marketing campaign lets consumers craft a personalized video that contained pictures and names extracted from their Facebook account. Recipients had to watch the touching video when they received a box of Cadbury glow chocolate, either via a QR code or by typing their phone number into the Cadbury glow page.

Figure 2-3 Cadbury GLOW | George Young's personalized video

Cadbury achieved a 65% click-through rate with recipients, in addition to a 33% conversion rate for viewers who filled in the following promotion form. The same year, Cadbury created a similar consumer-brand connection with a flavor matcher campaign targeting Australian customers.[15]

The main reasons why storytelling is an absolute necessity for branding:

- It builds a more profound and stronger connection with the consumer.
- It adds a human nature to the content and Increases Brand Recognition
- Storytelling goes beyond advertising; it makes brands more trustworthy.
- It lets businesses connect with customers in a divided and noisy media world.
- Stories help share a brand message; compelling stories go viral.
- A business with a great story can challenge its competitors easily.

- Stories are the most successful asset to create brand loyalty, making people more willing to promote a product or brand by word-of-mouth, which is the best way to popularize a business. 16

In a fantastic story around a soap, Dove decided to include men in its great storytelling approach to marketing https://bit.ly/3voAaZE. Dove's emotional story of being cared for and recognized makes a beautiful moment. For years Dove focused on real people and their stories, specifically women who are 'real,' as in not supermodels. Dove made its way by telling stories about beauty, whether it is the beauty of a mother and daughter relationship, or the beauty of a face and body generally viewed as an 'average.'17

Figure 2-4 #TakeTheTime | Dove Men+Care, Dove Men+Care is committed to supporting paternity leave in Canada.

In Summary, a successful good story is built around the consumer needs and should be:

- Contagious
- Personalized
- Self-actualization
- Engaging

- Easy to understand
- Emotive
- Believable
- Useful
- Inspiring
- Inclusive
- About a lifestyle experience

2.2 REFERENCES

1. Godin, S. (1999) *Permission Marketing: Turning Strangers into Friends and Friends into Customers*, Simon & Schuster; 1st edition, https://amzn.to/2U3Nzcf
2. Story, L. (2007, January 15), *Anywhere the Eye Can See, it is Likely to See an Ad*, https://nyti.ms/3pQ5E9G
3. Tankovska, H. (2021, February 8), *Daily time spent on social networking by internet users worldwide from 2012 to 2020*, https://bit.ly/3zptBsq
4. Statista (2021) *Social Media Advertising*, https://bit.ly/3vjJxJu
5. Asurion (2019, November 14), *Americans Check Their Phones 96 Times a Day*, https://bit.ly/3pMVjuO
6. Business wire (2011, April 28) *AOL Research: Content is the Fuel of the Social Web*, https://bwnews.pr/3iyRl7G
7. Fog, K., Budtz, C., Munch, P., Blanchette, B., (2010). *Storytelling Branding in Practice*. Springer; 2nd Edition, pp 22, 23, 231, https://amzn.to/3vm3LCu
8. McPherson, F., (2011), *The Role of Emotion in Memory*, https://bit.ly/2Sncozy
9. Brandt, D. (2017, February 22) *Understanding memory in advertising*, https://bit.ly/2U3smPJ
10. Pringle, H. (2008) *Brand Immortality*, Kogan Page; 1st edition, *pp 176*, https://amzn.to/3gfQFma

11. Dooley, R., (2009), *Emotional Ads Work Best*, https://bit.ly/3aNwXer
12. Kimberly A. (2018, July 14) *3 Reasons Why Storytelling Should Be a Priority for Marketers*, https://bit.ly/3wfjTHj
13. Accenture (2017) *U.S. consumers turn off personal data tap as companies struggle to deliver the experiences they crave, Accenture study finds*, https://accntu.re/3czghrF
14. Infosys (2014) *Rethinking retail insights from consumers and retailers into an omnichannel shopping experience* https://infy.com/3cFQGxp
15. Bullock, L., (2018, Dec 28) *5 Brands Taking Personalized Marketing to The Next Level*, https://bit.ly/3voBY4q
16. Bhattacharya, J., *7 Examples of storytelling content you can use in your marketing campaigns*, https://bit.ly/3zqXOYb
17. Ashraf, S. (2018, April 22) *7 incredible examples of brand storytelling on social media*, https://bit.ly/3oXjdDK

Chapter 3

3.1 THE ELEMENTS OF A STORY

A traditional story consists of the beginning, middle, and end. First, the scene is the set. Next, the progression of dynamic change creates conflict events and sets the parameters for the rest of the story. Plots describe the natural progression of escalating events. The conflict escalates but finally resolves, marking the end of the story. A brand storytelling content should include these:

- The hero who is a standard customer in a life journey facing challenges
- The Relatability of the story. When a customer becomes part of the story, puts himself in the hero's shoes, then responds to what the hero is confronting.
- The authenticity that generates empathy
- Story Setting where and when
- Curiosity, a reason to care or be curious.
- A message of purpose and goal
- A plot of cascading events
- A Conflict and struggles that reveal emotions or empathy.
- A satisfying resolution ending.

A story that customers can relate to that they can see themselves in will remain quicker in their memory than the story that starts with stats. A customer who may have a stubborn boss or face the same challenges with legal compliance might empathize with a hero who overcomes the same challenge or struggle. Therefore, marketers should not rely on the customer to interpret abstract information and concepts. Instead, they should tell the story of a similar person so the brain can visualize and experience the information vicariously. Relatability is essential when a customer puts himself in the hero's journey with any story. Humans are programmed to respond to stories that they can see themselves in by default. [1]

3.2 STORY BRAND PURPOSE AND GOAL

In his journey, the hero must undertake a conflict associated with struggle, risk, and danger to achieve a purpose he cares about to achieve the story's goal. If a hero has no goal, no need, there is no reason to struggle or face the conflicts and no reason to confront risk and danger. The purpose establishes a hero's story goal. All elements of the story are dependent upon the hero. The plot derives from hero and struggle. The beginning, the middle, and the end are made to serve the hero's needs, and the plot is the servant of the hero. The brand has goals that matter to the customers, and sharing these goals encourages them to engage with the brand to achieve and fulfilling the purpose. Passion must be the driving force behind the hero's pursuit. The company solution must strive to make a difference for the customer, who is the hero of the story facing struggles and obstacles in his buying journey.

"While traveling in Argentina in 2006, Blake Mycoskie TOMS Founder witnessed the hardships faced by children growing up without shoes. Wanting to help, he created TOMS Shoes, a company that would match every pair of shoes purchased with a new pair of shoes for a child in need. One for One®." Blake Mycoskie created the company, and its purpose and goal were in a bold, clear message within these three words" One for One®." 2

Figure 3-1 https://ourgoodbrands.com/one-for-one-model-started-revolutionary-business/

3.3 REFERENCES

1. Crossfield, J., (2019 April) *The Neuroscience of Storytelling,* https://bit.ly/3xaqvXA
2. Wachtel, T., (2020, December 15) *Brand Storytelling Is Not Just Important; It is Absolutely Critical,* https://bit.ly/3guy70m

Chapter 4

4.1 THE CONFLICT

The transcending message for a company's core story shall include a level of conflict within that message. What does the company stand for, and what it fights for to help its customers to thrive? Without a conflict, there is no story, and there is no meaning for that core message. In the context of branding, the conflicts are the obstacles customers want to conquer. Thus, a brand supports its consumers in the pursuit of their aspirations.

It is the conflict that creates the dynamics of a good story. The conflict is the barrier that the hero seeks to overcome to achieve the goal. Through this conflict, A brand can make its stand while expressing its core values simultaneously. Effectively, building contrasts and opposites are just like the battle between positive and negative experiences, sweet and sour, or fun versus dull. However, in business, a conflict is not necessarily a negative thing. Instead, it is the mechanism for creating a distinctive brand.

American movies over the years often used the good and evil conflict plot template for entertainment purposes. It is difficult to imagine a great film like Jaws without a hungry white shark, Superman without kryptonite, or the tale of Little Red Riding Hood without a fierce wolf. The teens would have had a wonderful summer at the beach, Superman would not have had a concern about the world, and Little Red Riding Hood would visit her grandmother and then go home. Boring and predictable events would not matter for anyone! No one would pay to watch a boring movie without conflict, and a fight between the good and the evil forces and goal never accomplished. Conflict is the motivating force of a good story. No conflict, no story. When faced with a problem or a conflict, the audience instinctively seeks to find a solution. Conflict forces people to act. The characters must be challenged to take action because human beings do not make significant life decisions unless something challenges them. In the classical fairytale story template, conflict expresses itself as a battle between good and evil: the hero versus the villain. The struggle between good and evil communicates the narrator's perspective, communicating their values and message to the audience. In storytelling, conflict is not harmful or a bad thing. On the contrary, it is a fundamental premise that the narrator can express their perception of right and wrong. Once a marketer decided on a possible transcending message for the brand core story, the next step is to assess the level of conflict within that message. How big a difference does a brand cause make, and what is it fighting to accomplish or help customers solve their problems?

4.2 THE OPPOSITE COUNTERPARTS

Developing a conflict is about defining two opposing forces or even more. For example, determining the complete opposite of a brand helps explain the brand's core story. Here are a few examples:

Apple:

Inclusion, diversity, and privacy ><Anonymous uniformity

Nike:

The will to win, inspiration, and innovation >< Losing

LEGO:

Creativity, imagination and learning >< Passive entertainment

Virgin:

Insatiable curiosity >< Business as usual

IKEA:

Cost-consciousness >< Design luxury for the few elite

Harley Davidson:

The excitement of freedom >< Boring daily routines

Without conflict, it is challenging to build and maintain a strong core story. If what a brand story is fighting for constitutes customer needs that have already been met, there is no solid adversary to drive the story forward. The world might say we would not need Nike if we were all born athletes winners. Marketers need to reassess purpose and where their brand is heading.

Dreams make a good motivator in a core story. Harley-Davidson is selling a dream; Harley-Davidson's concept of freedom contrasts with the norms that society places on people and the obligations that follow. The Harley-Davidson conflict lies in Life on the open road versus the straightjacket of "normal" life https://bit.ly/3ymLbvY. The conflict lies between freedom and routine daily activities, which appeals to much a symbol of Americana as Coca-Cola, Pepsi, all who believe in the American Dream. Harley-

Davidson is like McDonald's, and burger king in being part of the culture of society.

Figure 4-1 Harley-Davidson's, United We Will Ride

4.3 ADVERSARIES

Stories happen to characters, but they are about the problems and flowing events that story characters must face. Problems and struggles between the opposing forces are the elements that create conflict. When conflict becomes dangerous, it generates more suspense in its nature. Conflict implies adversaries. These opponents may be external or internal. They may be living beings or forces of nature. The risk and danger associated with the problems and flaws are what the audience cares about and wants to know. Characters must have an interest in the outcome of their struggles. They must have something at risk for which they struggle. There must be some danger to characters. This danger need not be physical. Threat to their motions, their reputation, or their self-image is every bit as valid and exciting. Suppose characters risk nothing, face no danger, and have nothing to lose. In that case, the audience will never feel compelled to stick around to see how the story comes out conflict.

4.4 STRUGGLES

Struggles are the actions a character takes to overcome conflict. No action (internal or external) means no story. Struggles require a hero and conflict to have meaning for the consumer. If the consumers put themselves in the hero's shoes, they become part of the story, and they definitely will engage and connect emotionally with story outcomes. [1]

4.1 REFERENCES

1. Fog, K., Budtz, C., Munch, P., Blanchette, B., (2010). *Storytelling Branding in Practice.* Springer; 2nd Edition, pp 34-41, https://amzn.to/3vm3LCu

Chapter 5

5.1 HERO

A story typically features a hero pursuing a goal. The hero looks like a Robin Hood fighting for justice and freedom in England. However, the hero's path to achieving his goal is not problem-free .The adversary tries to fight against the hero, thereby forming the conflict. In the viral Robin Hood story, the adversaries are Prince John and the Sheriff of Nottingham, who must be eliminated for justice to prevail.

A traditional story emerges into three parts: beginning, middle, and end. The events' progression and escalation create conflict and set the boundaries for the rest of the story. When the conflict escalates to the tipping point, it is finally resolved, marking the end of the story. A successful conflict requires a hero and a villain with opposing goals. In the hero's journey, the adversary stands in opposition to the hero's pursuit. By fighting against the adversary, the hero struggles toward his personal development and resolves the story's conflict. To get customers involved in a story, marketers must interact with the characters similar as readers or listeners, or viewers, especially when they see a little bit of themselves in the characters in the story identifying the character's problem and goal. For a successful story, the audience must engage with both the hero and the story's dilemma.[1]

One of the big modern-day corporate conflict stories is Steve Jobs returning to Apple after being terminated from his established company. It is a "Voyage and Return" plot story. What makes Steve Jobs return so compelling is the setting/the time. Apple was in trouble, and its innovation driving force has stopped. Returning to his visionary roots, his time away from Apple in Pixar movies contributed to the turnaround. Steve learned at Pixar the strength of story visualization and how that impacts the audience. He applied storytelling visualization in announcing to the world Apple's first smartphone https://bit.ly/3jmtHfd. Steve Jobs was motivated to make a change, and he successfully and brilliantly did a profound shift that affected the whole world by Apple's innovative product, the smartphone.

Figure 5-1 Steve Jobs Introduces the iPhone to the World 2007

The fatal mistake some brands make, incredibly immature new brands who believe they need to prove themselves, are positioning themselves as heroes in the story instead of the guide. A brand that sets itself as the hero is to lose unless there is a clear purpose.

Domino's Pizza, a brand once afflicted by poor customer opinions of its quality. In a series of ad campaigns, the company explicitly acknowledged these complaints and announced efforts to improve. Dominos had to revive the brand. Dominos launched an ad campaign that has become legendary for its courage, sharing comments in social media from focus groups about what people thought of the product: "worst pizza I ever had"; "the sauce tastes like ketchup"; "the crust tastes like cardboard." [2] They even created a "Pizza Turnaround" documentary to commemorate the process https://bit.ly/3aU5hog.Since then, their sales have grown substantially. Domino's Pizza announced the first quarter of 2021 financial results showing a global growth of 14% despite the pandemic Covid 2019. [3] In this successful brand storytelling effort, Domino's leveraged all three elements in its favor: The character of a brand invested in customer satisfaction, the conflict with consumer disappointment, and the conclusion of making good on a renewed commitment to quality. The story's purpose is that brand is caring and courageous about earning the satisfaction of its customers.[4] The critical point is to focus on the customers, offering them a heroic role in a meaningful remembered story. Customers need to be heard, understood with the essence of empathy. Genuine empathy means letting customers know that brands see them and sympathize with them.

Figure 5-2 Domino's® Pizza Turnaround

5.2 THE HERO JOURNEY

A hero character is the central organizing element of all stories. Stories occur to characters who are the driving force of a story, but not all stories are worth telling unless they have meaning and purpose. Sometimes, a brand may serve as a character hero, but there should be a valid reason to explain a goal or purpose around the character facing a problem. For example, it is better off to make a customer the hero of the brand story, telling stories about issues customers have met, stories about customers who look like customers, and stories that customers can imagine themselves in.

A brand story is a narrative that illustrates its origins, exposes why a brand exists, and the problem it solves for its customers in their struggle to find a solution to their problems. It resonates with the customer and attracts them towards brand values and core messages, even if they are not explicitly stated in the story. The hero takes the actions, experiences the conflicts, and undertakes the struggles of a story. Hero is at the core of every story element and event. No other element has meaning and relevance without a hero seeking a meaningful goal taking risks and overcoming conflicts and struggles. When a customer is a hero in the story, the product or service plays the supporting and guiding role, which helps the customer finds a solution or accomplish a goal. The hero character adds flesh and blood to the brand's role in the story world. On the other hand, it also sheds light on the conflict and the passion that motivates the brand to advance. 5

5.3 REFERENCES

1. Fog, K., Budtz, C., Munch, P., Blanchette, B., (2010). *Storytelling Branding in Practice. Springer*; 2nd Edition, pp 22, 23, 231, https://amzn.to/3vm3LCu
2. Taylor, B. (2016, November 28) *How Domino's Pizza Reinvented Itself,* https://bit.ly/3zMO6zA
3. PRNewswire (2021), *Domino's Pizza® Announces First Quarter 2021 Financial Results,* https://prn.to/3qlc14O
4. Brandtrust (2018, January 25), *Your Brand Storytelling Checklist: Everything You Need to Craft Your Brand's Story,* https://brandtrust.com/blog/brand-storytelling/
5. Miller, D. (2017) *Building a StoryBrand: Clarify Your Message So Customers Will Listen*, HarperCollins Leadership, pp. 96, https://amzn.to/2RLERhU

Chapter 6

6.1 THE PLOT

The plot is an essential part of any story as it escalates the events in a hero's journey in a logical order. It defines what the story is all about, what the hero will experience, and what it will achieve. It sets up the motivations, challenges, the goal, and the road hero takes to fulfill it. Once a message, conflict, and cast of characters are all in place, the plot starts the progress of the events. Story flowing events are vital to the audience's experience. A story only occurs as a progression of sequence events within a given time at a set location that needs careful consideration. It must have a coherent composition to propel it forward and maintain audience interest. Once the conflict escalates to no return point, the hero decides, influencing the outcome result. The escalation of the conflict and the hero's character progress development drives the story forward, building up to a climax, where the hero finally confronts the villain.[1] The seven basic plots: Why We Tell Stories is a 2004 book by Christopher Booker, contained an influenced analysis of story plots and their psychological meaning.[2] The seven plots are as follows:-

1) **Overcoming the monster**
   It was featured in James Bond, Jaws, and many other movies. This plot is about a hero and an evil force. In a real-world example, this could be overcoming an addiction, fighting off a lousy boss, debt, beating an illness, or anything else that

requires something to be defeated for the hero (customer) to win.

2) **Rags to riches**
Like Cinderella and Aladdin, the success and crisis apply to anyone with an undeniably incredible talent who wants to break through and be successful in the real world, i.e., Photographers, musicians, artists, authors like Harry Potter J. K. Rowling.

3) **The Quest**
Lord of the Rings, seeking and finding. This is indeed the story of every beginning entrepreneurial journey—a product or service to be a long-lasting tool that can last along the way.

4) **Voyage and return**
The Time Machine exploring. Alice in wonderland. A brand assists the customer at their arrival destination. It could be language learning software, cultural etiquette training, photo guides, maps, and tours.

5) **Comedy**
Bridget Jones's Diary. From confusion to enlightenment. The comedy plot involves confusion that must be resolved before the hero and heroine can be united in love.

In the real world, customers cannot seem to get out of their way. They are constantly finding themselves in one misadventure after another and could use a little assistance (the brand) to be lead on the right path.

6) **Tragedy**
Romeo and Juliet, the price of fatal flaws.

Plots about divorce lawyers, grief counselors, self-help books, and anyone who helps their customer get through a tough time. Because this is so self-evident, it is not difficult to identify when a customer is going through a tragedy.

7) **Rebirth**

They are finding the personal light. But, unfortunately, in the real world, just like in "A Christmas Carol," customers may not even know a problem exists until a brand shows them just how bad they were doing.

In most Hollywood films, screenwriters used these seven plot templates to build up their stories which often end positively, restoring harmony. Most plots revolve around a hero fighting evil, encountering a challenge, profound transformation in the hero's character due to unpleasant or sudden shocking events, or a hero pursuing a dream comes true.

6.2 ROBIN HOOD AND CAUSE MARKETING PLOT TEMPLATE

The company fights for justice. A brand is not afraid to battle against the dominating forces in the market: forces that have created a monopoly, which does not benefit the consumer. 70 % of consumers want brands to stand on social and political issues. That is a 66% increase from 2017, according to (Sprout Social's 2019) #BrandsGetReal survey. Following in the footprints of Nike and Patagonia, the list of brands holding social and political stands has grown to reach over every industry.

Consumers' social media feeds have recently become saturated with brands joining social justice conversations. However, consumers reported that brands do not always seem genuine, even before the Black Lives Matter movement. 53 % of consumers believe brands shall take a stand for P.R. and marketing purposes (known as [woke-washing](#)), and 35 % perceive brands speaking out as "jumping on the bandwagon." Brands should not be scared to take a stance, but they will need to sustain their credibility.

According to consumers surveyed by (Sprout Social 2019), a brand's stand is most believable when it is about an issue that impacts its customers and is relevant to the business. And it does not end there, and a company will also need to be clear about what it is doing to back its messaging by action. When consumers agree with a brand's stance, 37% will recommend that company to their friends and family, and 36% will buy more from that brand. Brands influencing the cause marketing technique, it is essential that they are transparent. Brands must prove a genuine commitment to the cause they are supporting, and this commitment needs to be examined along the whole customer journey. If brands genuinely consider making a difference by taking a social and political stand, understanding, and aligning with consumers' best interests is vital for creating a successful campaign and powerful results. [3](#)

6.2.1.1 Mastercard Tried to and failed

Mastercard launched a similarly out-of-touch campaign as part of the 2018 FIFA World Cup. The brand proposed to donate 10,000 meals to starving in developing countries for every goal scored by Messi or Neymar Jr in the international tournament. It caused an immediate social protest, indicating that the multi-billion-dollar company donated the meals regardless of which players scored. Eventually, Mastercard admitted and agreed that it would donate the meals, yet was left red-faced, proof that specific topics, such as starving children, should be tackled very properly in marketing campaigns to avoid backfire.

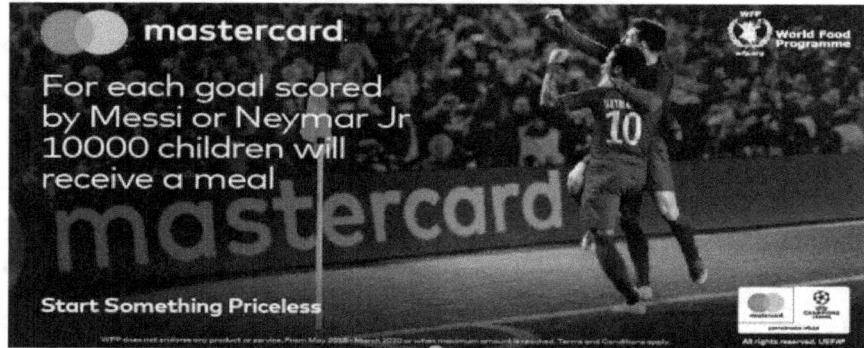

Figure 6-1 https://www.thedrum.com/news/2019/06/19/cause-marketing-best-and-worst-brand-purpose-campaigns

6.2.1.2   Airbnb Weaccept

After President Trump temporarily blocked America's borders to refugees, Airbnb aired a Super Bowl ad to criticize the order, called "We Accept." Airbnb also promised to provide short-term housing for 100,000 displaced people and donate $4 million to the International Rescue Committee. Their campaign "Acceptance starts with all of us #weaccept" 4 was a well-received campaign by the audience, marking a significant impact https://bit.ly/3xG2IQi .5

THE ART OF BRAND STORYTELLING

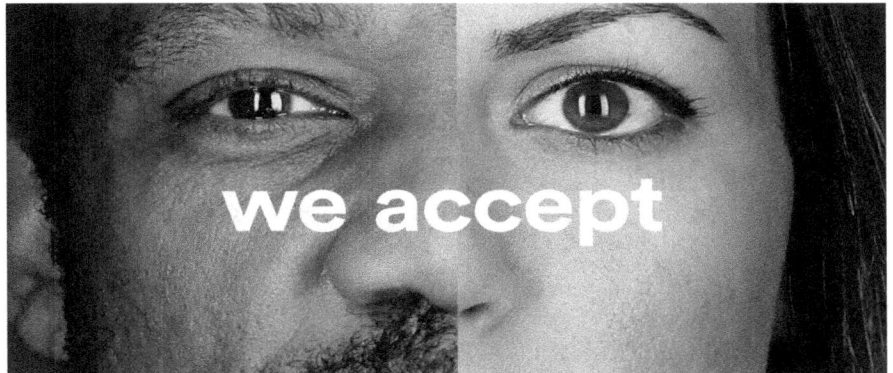

Figure 6-2 Super Bowl Airbnb's ad celebrates acceptance

6.2.1.3 Luna Bar Women rights for equal pay

Luna nutrition bar aimed at and founded supporting issues like women's rights for equal pay. The food LUNA makes is crafted with purpose. The bars are non-GMO, gluten-free, and made with organic rolled oats. Realizing their female consumer base prospective shared similar values, LUNA® Bar saw an opportunity to attract the female consumer segment interested in diets and organic nutrition by raising awareness around gender equality.

Figure 6-3 https://www.instagram.com/lunabar/?hl=en

6.3 SUSTAINABILITY PLOT TEMPLATE

Like the quest plot, the company started as the black horse in the market that nobody thought would ever accomplish anything. It becomes a force in its qualities and skills, surprising and impressing even its harshest critics. All companies have the authentic raw material for telling their own stories.

Marketers shall build a corporate brand on the real-life stories told by the employees, customers, and working partners. Stories anchored in the corporate culture create a solid and authentic brand for a company. Clothing brands like Patagonia and The North Face have consistently supported causes that work to protect the environment. Patagonia's campaigns have always helped the brand's environmental vows; all the profits made over 2016's Black Friday sale were donated entirely to local environmental NGOs. Moreover, Patagonia's subversive 'Don't buy this jacket' campaign helped raise awareness over the dangers of fast fashion and the importance of recycling clothing.6

Figure 6-4 https://www.thedrum.com/news/2017/02/22/why-patagonias-the-wall-advertising-asks-customers-think-twice-buying-its-products

6.4 REFERENCES

1. Fog, K., Budtz, C., Munch, P., Blanchette, B., (2010). Storytelling Branding in Practice. Springer; 2nd Edition, pp 22, 23, 231, https://amzn.to/3vm3LCu
2. Booker, C. (2006) *The Seven Basic Plots, Continuum*, 1st edition, p 229-233, https://amzn.to/3x4HzOZ
3. Social sprout (2019), *#BrandsGetReal: Brands Creating Change in the Conscious Consumer Era*, https://bit.ly/3qqFzOx
4. YouTube (2021)Airbnb#weaccept https://bit.ly/3dTZxMz
5. Wren, H., (2020, December 23) *6 companies tackling social justice and inspiring customers*, https://bit.ly/2Uc4Lfu
6. Mulcahy, E., (2019, June 21) *Cause marketing: examples of the best and worst brand purpose campaigns* https://bit.ly/3gZ3HEM

Chapter 7

7.1 THE VILLAIN

Every great hero needs a great villain. Villains are the opposing force of a story that challenges the hero and drives the action. A good villain is a complex evil character whom readers and viewers simultaneously love and hate. Unless marketers define the brand's villains, the hero will not stand out brightly. Stories with heroes and villains might inspire the customers to change. The Audience empathizes and mimics heroes' behavior and suppresses the behaviors embodied by villains. A good villain makes a story a lot more entertaining and exciting for the viewers as it keeps the suspense growing across the progression of story events. Villains and adversaries give context to the story plot in a way that no other character can do because they make the audience see the level of evil or opposition through the hero's eyes. Villains in the content marketing perspective often are not people or objects. Customer frustration, overpricing, confusing processes, terrible customer support, slow service, and the complicated purchasing process could be the adversary forces of antagonism that a heroic brand shall conquer. According to (Sprout's 2017) research, 66% of respondents felt it is essential for brands to take a public stance on leading social and political issues like immigration, human rights, and race relations. Marketers can use these causes to invent an adversary force in brand storytelling. [1]

7.2 SOUTHWEST AIRLINES "TRANSFARENCY"

Southwest Airlines builds its pricing model around the villain of competitors' hidden fees. The Carrier celebrated customers and underscored core values such as low fares. While other low-cost airlines charge for seat choices, checked bags, and even water, Southwest does not. In 2015, Southwest Airlines launched the "Transfarency" campaign focused on the carrier's low-fare message and newly refreshed livery and interior. The 2017 campaign -Behind Every Story is the Reason for Transfarency- built on Transfarency through the emotional telling of customer stories and their reasons for flying. They reminded customers that they were at the core of the carrier's purpose: connect passengers to what is essential in their lives through friendly, reliable, and low-cost air travel. They made up a unique trust for their no-hidden-fees pricing strategy: "Transfarency," which is a philosophy of treating customers honestly and fairly, and low fares stay low—no unexpected bag fees, change fees, or hidden fees. Low fares. No hidden fees. Southwest Airlines created this villain in their marketing all the time, and people like it and engage with it https://bit.ly/3nl6mEP. 2

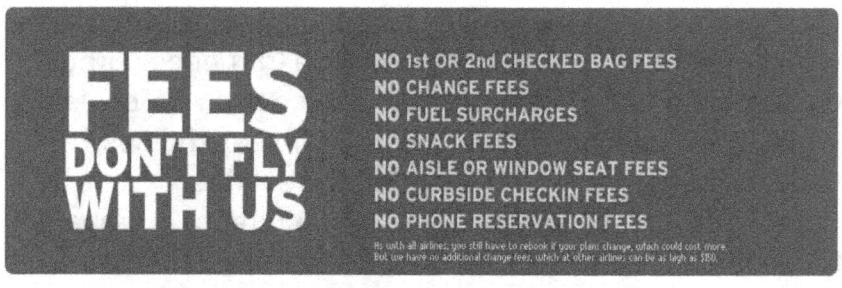
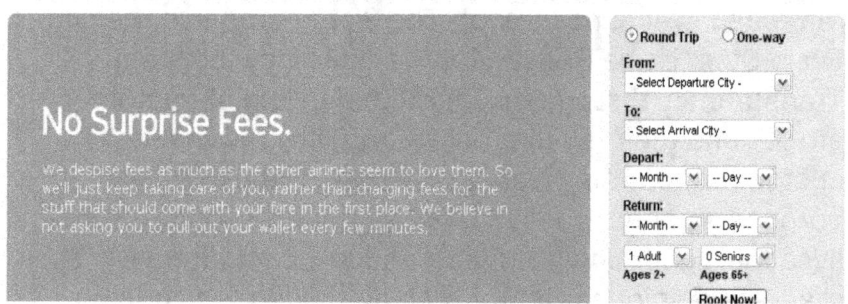

Figure 7-1 https://www.southwest.com/

7.3 REFERENCES

1. Sprout Social (2017) *#BrandsGetReal: Championing Change in the Age of Social Media,*
https://bit.ly/3wVEUqv
2. Prnewswire (2017) *Behind Every Seat Is a Story: Southwest Airlines Launches Next Phase of Transfarency Consumer Campaign,*
https://prn.to/3x1T9uj

Chapter 8

8.1 A PURPOSE CORPORATE CORE MESSAGE STORY

At the corporate level, a brand core story revolves around values connects with an audience with similar values and beliefs, which invites them to become brand loyal tribes. A purpose message surrounding a brand helps shape a company's identity if it uses storytelling narrative techniques that enable an emotional response from the audience and make meaningful connections. The message should not be confused with a slogan or logo. A tagline is a short, catchy expression that incorporates the story message used in company advertising.

Brand storytelling is a tool for telling stories, not for its sake. Instead, marketers used stories to deliver messages positively to the company brand. But what is a well-defined message? Without a strategic purpose, there is no reason to tell stories. For example, "Just Do It" is Nike's slogan; however, their message is that every game is about winning. With effort and determination, everyone can be a winner. Nike is fighting to help the customers be more confident about themselves, overcome restraints, and "Just Do It" to win. Nike is fighting a lack of self-confidence and hesitation. According to Nike, if anyone wants to win, quitting is not an option, and reaching a goal might require sacrifice.[1]

8.2 BELIEVE IN SOMETHING, EVEN IF IT MEANS SACRIFICING EVERYTHING

In a Nike controversial commercial IN 2018, Colin Kaepernick focused on sacrificing moto initiated a vast debate in social media between the audience who split between disagreed and agreed on that message: https://bit.ly/3ekRbOE. Although Nike lost a slice of its angry customers, Nike successfully received a large scale of brand recognition created all over the news and in harsh debates between potential consumers. The controversial Ad won the award for outstanding commercial at the Creative Arts Emmys.[2] According to Business Insider, the ad was successful, despite its high risk. It was trending on Twitter for millions; Nike received more than $43 million worth of media exposure, nearly $19 million worth of which was positive. Nike fully invested in the cause and the heroism that Kaepernick portrayed. That heroism role was the essential part of Robin Hood storytelling ad confronting the adversary forces of disagreed Trump supporters during the escalation of conflict events. Nike saw an opportunity of polarization throughout divided America then used it as a marketing tool. Despite the backfire from some Americans, the campaign was a successful hit. Nike Stocks rose by 5% in the weeks following the ad's release. [3]

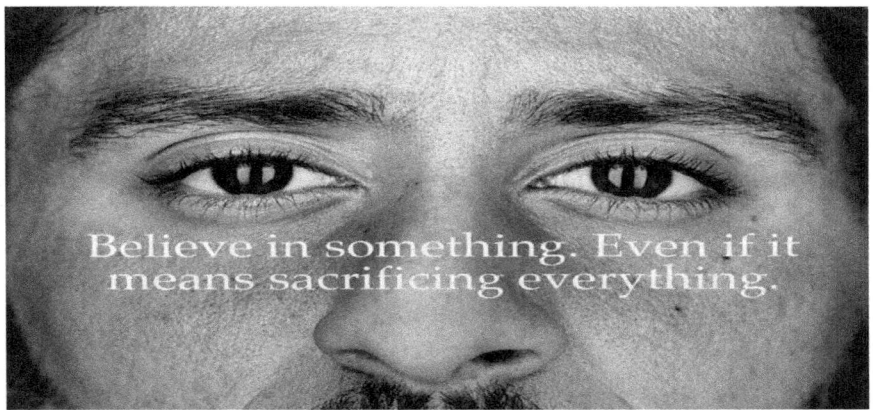

Figure 8-1 Kaepernick's Nike ad.

8.3 FOREVER AGAINST ANIMAL TESTING: JOIN THE FIGHT!

The possibility for animal testing is still a massive risk worldwide—no laws against testing in cosmetics in over 80% of countries. Cruelty-Free International estimates that approximately 500,000 animals are still used in cosmetics testing every year. Anita Roddick established the Body Shop beauty brand in 1976. The founder wanted her company to stand for important values associated with brand identity. An important message accompanied the brand, launched by an alliance with internal employees and customers in 1989. The Body Shop, which has over 3,000 stores in more than 60 countries, was the first international cosmetic brand to campaign against animal testing in cosmetics in 1989, opening the way to a U.K. ban in 1998 and a European Union-wide ban on animal testing in 2013 https://bit.ly/3b6PUcb. The Body Shop continues its efforts to fight passionately against animal testing on products and ingredients, which is cruel and unnecessary. 4

The Body Shop implemented a Robin hood storytelling plot fighting for animals against the adversary forces of greedy unworried competitors. The brand usefully delivered its message and won in some ethical battles.

Figure 8-2 https://thebodyshop.com.kh/en/forever-against-animal-testing

8.4 "SUSTAINABILITY IS NOW AS IMPORTANT AS SAFETY TO US"

Håkan Samuelsson, Chief Executive Volvo Cars

Since the beginning, Volvo started as a car brand associated with safety as a purpose-based company https://bit.ly/3etrR9q. Volvo is always proud of its invention, the 3-point safety belt, and the millions of lives it saved over the years. Volvo waived its patent rights to allow other car

manufacturers to use this technology
https://bit.ly/3nXLpFP.

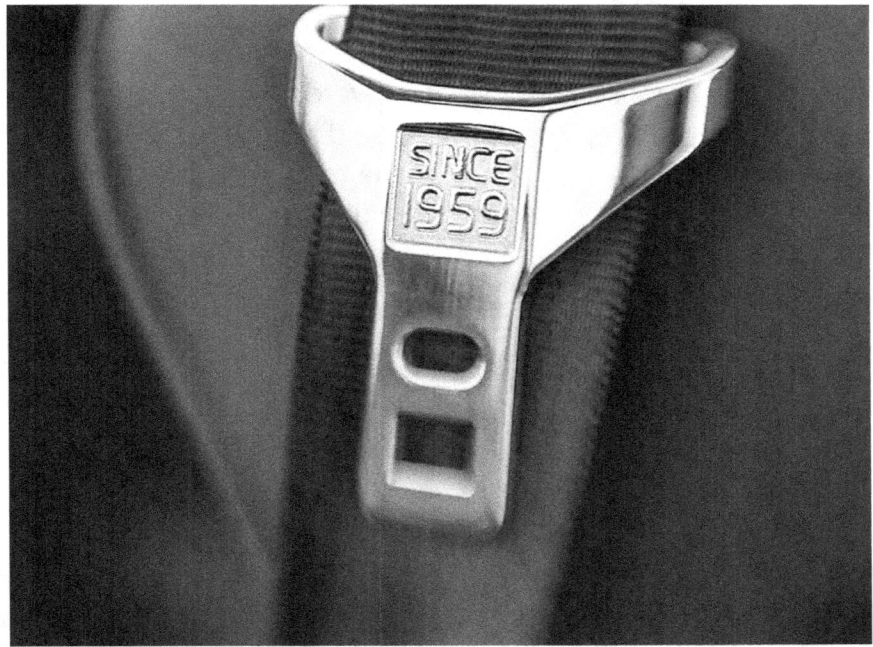

Figure 8-3 https://www.volvocars.com/intl/v/car-safety/a-million-more

In 2021 Volvo changed its direction towards electric cars and green energy as a sustainable strategy towards the future. Volvo's ambition is to become a fully electric car company by 2030 and climate neutral by 2040." Sustainability is now as vital as safety to us, and climate change is the ultimate safety test." The CEO of Volvo cars announced this direction of the company in a YouTube video, "Volvo Cars Moment: Recharge " https://bit.ly/2SDPweV with the hashtag #ForEveryonesSafety. The company posted a catchy ad, "The Ultimate Safety Test," to emphasize to its customers and the world that the biggest threat to safety now comes from climate change. In the new ad, a spokesperson called 'Bjorn' takes viewers on a tour of Volvo's safety tests over the years and then moves up north to the arctic pole, where he asked whether a 100-foot drop is suitable as the ultimate safety test. A collapsing glacier delivered the shocking answer, interrupting the ad with a bold reminder that the biggest threat to safety is not on the road. According to Volvo, today, climate change is the ultimate safety test [5]. Volvo currently cares about climate change as a brand purpose alongside safety https://bit.ly/3exWmLv.[6]

Figure 8-4 https://www.volvocars.com/mt/why-volvo/human-innovation/future-of-driving/the-ultimate-safety-test

8.5 BOSCH REVOLVES AROUND THE "INVENTED FOR LIFE"

The contagious shift towards sustainability also affected the giant German engineering company. Bosch ranked 77 in the Fortune Global (100) in 2020.[7] The company is well known for its quality, precision, innovative strength, and connection between technology with people, its brand core purpose message "Invented For Life." The evolution of IoT-Internet of Things- The reality of "connected devices" led Bosch to pursue a new brand identity to take their place in the evolving world. As a result, the brand had to redefine the meaning of its "Invented For Life" claim and change its core value messaging and identity to make a direct emotional connection with its variety of consumers throughout both b2b and b2c channels and platforms.[8] The Covid-19 pandemic accelerated the company shift towards digitalization, creativity, technology, and climate change sustainability https://bit.ly/3f52MjV, "Shifting paradigms: Creativity. Technology. Trust".

The company's CEO Dr. Volkmar Dennner appeared in a YouTube video to talk about Bosch's core values and its messaging to the world. "Despite all the changes, one success factor remains the same: people. For Bosch, people have the final say. They stay in control. Technology remains explainable because we must be able to trust it. It is the only way to build openness and acceptance for tomorrow's technologies created by people for people and a better world. Or, as we put it at Bosch: Invented for life". From washing machines, dishwashers, and e-drives to drilling tools—Bosch is improving products that enhance the quality of life, which help preserve natural resources. Also, the company started reducing its carbon footprint a long time ago. It achieved CO_2 neutrality at its over 400 locations worldwide in 2020—making it the first global industrial company to do so. Bosch took sustainability seriously and presented live sustainable #LikeABosch https://bit.ly/33rlDk6. 9

Figure 8-5 https://www.bosch.com/stories/sustainability-likeabosch/

8.6 DOING IT RIGHT AT FIRST TIME WITH CONSTANT CARE

At Danish shipping company A.P. Moller - Maersk Group, the central message has always been that trust, connection, people, discipline, punctuality, disciplined execution, and constant care. Every time the company is paying attention to detail, doing it right for the first time is the foundation of a reliable business https://bit.ly/3f5hmlb. In return, their customers can be safe knowing that things are always on track. The passed away founder of the company MC Kinney Moller used to express his message in two words "constant care," a term that, to this day, is firmly rooted at the heart of the company and its core story.10

Figure 8-6 Emma Maersk (Photo: Maersk Line)

"Imagine if a restaurant was like shipping" https://bit.ly/3hQFWy2 is an ad by Maersk featuring a story clip inside a restaurant. The customers are the heroes and the victims, simultaneously facing a conflict of overbooking, price rise, and uncertainty of their orders. A couple was rolled out of the restaurant on a rainy night due to complex overbooking. The company emphasized its solution to the problem by introducing Maersk spot, loading guarantee, easy online booking, and fixed price, https://www.maersk.com/spot. The company continues to deliver more core messages around its brand core values.

Here are some more inspirational examples of other brand's core stories:

Harley-Davidson is about independence and power, freedom to travel, living a life without rules.

Apple is about innovation and shaping technology to benefit human needs and recently added privacy.

Greenpeace is battling for the global environment.

Virgin is about being playful, modern, and energetic.

LEGO is about kids' imagination, creativity, fun, learning, caring, quality, people promise, play.

Adidas builds on a passion for sports and a sporting lifestyle.

Pepsi is about "Excitement of Now."

Coca-Cola is about to "refresh the world in mind, body, and spirit, and inspire moments of optimism; to create value and make a difference."

BMW's is about sophistication.

Ford's is about "to make people's lives better by making mobility accessible and affordable."

Uber is beyond simple.

Redbull is about energy, boldness, adrenaline, actions, and adventures.

Ikea is about 'to offer a wide range of well-designed, functional home furnishing products at prices so low that as many people as possible will afford them.'

8.7 UNITED BREAKS THE GUITAR

United airlines write on its website: "We are committed to providing a level of service to our customers that makes us a leader in the airline industry. We understand that we need to have a proud product and employees who like coming to work every day. Our goal is to make every flight a positive experience for our customers". 11

When a company contradicts its values and commitment towards its customers, it is a severe problem. United airlines faced two major public relations disasters. The first one," united breaks the guitar," in 2009. The second one was more brutal in 2017 when a passenger violently dragged off the plane to free up seats for dead-heading employees. The core message of these two stories is that a brand did not learn from its past mistakes and continued to mistreat its customers taking benefits from a non-availability of enough competition in the U.S. airline industry. When a brand feels some monopoly over its market, it does not care anymore.

Musician Dave Carroll filed a complaint about his guitar, mishandled and broken while in United Airline's custody in 2008. The company refused to compensate or take any responsibility, which eventually led Carrol to publish a song on YouTube in 2009 https://bit.ly/33tXIjW about his horrible experience traveling with united airlines. The video went viral and passed 150,000 views within one day, prompting United to contact Carroll to say it hoped to correct the matter. The video had 5 million views by August 2009, 10 million by February 2011, and 15 million by August 2015. It has roughly 20.7 million views and 212,000 likes as of July 2021. Within four weeks of the video being posted online, United Airlines' stock price fell 10%, costing stockholders about $180 million in value. 12

Figure 8-7 https://www.nytimes.com/2009/10/29/business/29air.html

The second biggest P.R. crisis occurred in 2017. Dr. David Dao Duy Anh, a Vietnamese American passenger, was injured while being forcibly removed from a fully boarded, sold-out flight to Louisville International Airport. The incident Video went viral, and United Airlines stock plummeted. The company mishandled the incident, and the CEO issued two apology letters as the first one was bad. As a result, United's consumer perception dropped to a 10-year low. A consistent lousy reputation is difficult to recover despite aggressive marketing, brand building, and corporate storytelling messages [13].

A company without respecting and fulfilling its purpose core values and actions will not positively affect the business environment. A corporate core story must be strengthened and anchored throughout the company and integrated across all departments and sections to enhance brand identity internally and externally. Without a consistently excellent customer service experience, a brand loses its credibility and trustworthiness.

THE ART OF BRAND STORYTELLING

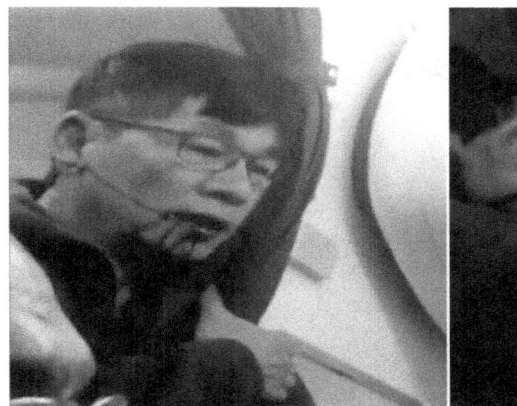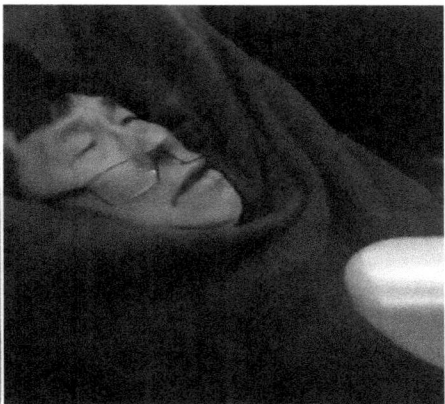

Figure 8-8 https://nypost.com/2017/04/12/the-surprising-past-career-of-the-dragged-united-passenger/

8.8 REFERENCES

1. Fog, K., Budtz, C., Munch, P., Blanchette, B., (2010). *Storytelling Branding in Practice*. Springer; 2nd Edition https://amzn.to/3vm3LCu
2. Guardian sport (2019) *Nike's 'Dream Crazy' advert starring Colin Kaepernick wins Emmy*, https://bit.ly/3x2Ta1d
3. Panichelli, J. (2018, September 11) *Would Nike sacrifice everything*, https://bit.ly/2TeVYcO
4. Newswire (2017) *The Body Shop and Cruelty-Free International Campaign to end cosmetic product and ingredient animal testing globally once and for all*, https://bit.ly/3eZxZFn
5. The Drum (2021) Volvo: *Ultimate Safety Test by Grey*, https://bit.ly/3xXkZJ9
6. Volvocars (2021) *Climate change is The Ultimate Safety*, https://bit.ly/2PXVeHk
7. Rankingthebrands(2020), The Ranking The Brands Top 100 https://bit.ly/2PXvuuC

8. Live sustainable #LikeABosch, https://bit.ly/3tyqc6t
9. Futurebrand (2021) Bosch invented for life
   https://bit.ly/2R21vlS
10. Maersk (2021) *Maersk Core Values,*
    https://bit.ly/3b9i6ew
11. United (2021) *Our United Customer Commitment,*
    https://bit.ly/3h9IPvf
12. Wikipedia (2021) *United Breaks Guitars,*
    https://en.wikipedia.org/wiki/United_Breaks_Guitars
13. Wikipedia (2021) *United Express Flight 3411 incident,*
    https://bit.ly/33uT854

Chapter 9

9.1 DIFFERENCE BETWEEN CASE STUDIES AND STORIES

There is a big difference between a case study and a story. Case studies are rough, rational raw materials that need to be formed into a story shape to make an emotional impact. Case studies are made of logic, facts, and numbers. These facts and figures cannot bond with an audience without a story, especially on the emotional level. [1] Marketers and advertisers are highly aware of the power of applying emotional storytelling to make a sufficient impact on customers to encourage or influence them to make an action or change their purchasing decisions behaviors.

Facts and logical information messages do not affect the customers who are bombarded daily with thousands of similar messages, so case studies' analytical information is quickly forgotten. Emotion messages and stories can capture customers' attention much longer than case studies and are more attached to the memories. When emotion is activated, the brain stores as many details as possible about the related event and prepares for quick recall of the information. Backed by solid emotion, memory can often pop up instantly, even years or decades after the event. Recalling these events can bring to mind the full spectrum of human emotion, from joy to fear, anger, or grief. The concept of emotional memory helps clarify why some memories can stay fresh in human minds for years while other memories become blurry and eventually fade. Emotion is the anchor that holds memories in humans' minds. Memorable events in someone's life often become anchored in the brain in "event clusters" like episodes of a story. Brands shall build their core stories to induce positive feelings in their consumer's subconscious, thus keeping them connected and attached to brands' messages even years after released advertising messages.[2]

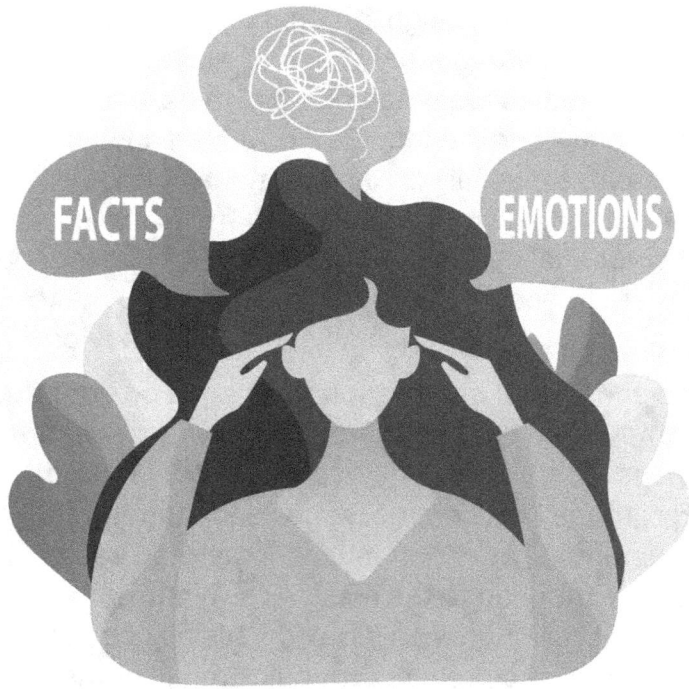

Figure 9-1 Facts and figures cannot bond with an audience without a story

Most companies have the raw material for telling stories, such as customer testimonials, real-life stories told by the employees, customers, and working partners. These raw materials can be easily shaped into stories to feed the corporate culture and core values. These corporate culture anchored stories create a solid and authentic brand foundation.

Figure 9-2 Corporate culture anchored stories create a solid and authentic brand foundation.

9.2 DOVE REAL BEAUTY SKETCHES, YOU'RE MORE BEAUTIFUL THAN YOU THINK

According to statistics, only 4% of women feel good about themselves worldwide. Dove did something that would move the other 96%. Dove investigated these figures and thought about an idea to prove that majority of women are wrong about their self-image. Dove shaped this idea into a storytelling ad just in YouTube video-https://bit.ly/33RsrYx made over 69.5 million views and thousands of comments and engagement. 2 In 2013, Dove, the soap brand company, posted ads featuring women who were the subjects of an FBI-trained forensic artist. Without seeing these women, the artist drew every woman individually based on her description. Soon After, the artist drew the same woman based on a stranger's description. The result was astonishing. The sketches drawn from the stranger's description were always more beautiful than those in which the women depicted themselves. Many women do not realize how beautiful they are. The ad attempted to help women accept themselves and find greater happiness in their intrinsic beauty.[3]

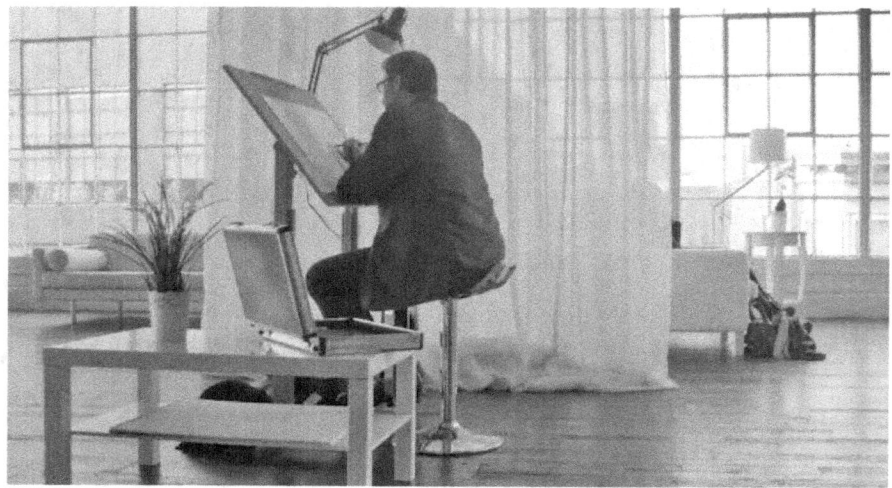

Figure 9-3 Dove Real Beauty Sketches | You're more beautiful than you think

Whether by fulfilling some purpose or accepting themselves as they are, the story resolves the internal conflict in human minds: the desire for self-acceptance. Many ads do not carry emotional stories; it markets a particular product or service benefit starring the brand as a superhero. These ads are a waste of effort and money.

Brands like Nike, Adidas, Red Bull, Rolex, Under Armour, Tiger Woods, Unilever, Coca Cola, and Porsche developed athletic and intellectual accomplishments and a sense of self-actualization.4 Brands realize how much sports fans love their sports heroes and will put up much money to get their brands in front of those cheering and passionate fans. If athletes who worked for their entire lives to achieve valuable objectives and meanings can achieve something, this purpose can be associated with the core aspect of a brand promise then transferred to the fans. 5

Figure 9-4 https://blog.hollywoodbranded.com/the-top-10-highest-endorsed-athletes-and-their-brands

9.3 REFERENCES

1. Dolan, G. (2017, May 1) *Stories for Work: The Essential Guide to Business Storytelling* Wiley; 1st edition Page 23, https://amzn.to/3AkbNjd
2. Overlook-mass (2017, April 21), *Differences Between Emotional Memory and Event memory*, https://bit.ly/3hs5ZND
3. Grose, J. (2013, April 19) *The Story Behind Dove's Mega Viral "Real Beauty Sketches" Campaign*, https://bit.ly/33AOuT7

4. Henry, A.J. (2021, May 3) *Pop Culture Brand Partnership News and Insights*, https://bit.ly/3y9rVmk
5. Miller, D. (2017) *Building a StoryBrand: Clarify Your Message So Customers Will Listen,* HarperCollins Leadership, https://amzn.to/2RLERhU

Chapter 10

10.1 APPLY THE STORY MODEL

When marketers want to create a brand's story, they need to set up the purpose, objectives, problems, and conflicts, assign heroes and villains, convey the plot climax, and then close with a satisfying ending to a narrative tailored to customer perception. A mere frustration is a recognizable villain of evil in the consumer's mind. The story problem starts from faulty products to cold coffee to melted ice cream to lousy customer service or a lengthy purchasing process or unjustified higher prices. All the story characters need a name, identity, and recognition. The victim and the hero are the customers whose brand must resolve their problems and make them satisfied and comfortable. When telling a story, customers' difficulties are apparent, and the escalation events will end with a brands' solution. Let "villains" come from the audience's perspective, so they recognize themselves as heroes. A brand product or service would act as the hero's guide in the consumer struggle journey for a satisfying happy ending solution that ends up their problems and frustration.

10.2 BRAND STORYTELLING MODEL

A story must be remarkable, emotional, and authentic to inspire the customers to push them to consider buying a brand and keep them as loyal fans. A brand must help them step further towards their dream and feel they are not alone because both fights for the same values and cause.

Industry	"Villain(s)"	"Hero(s)"	"Solution(s)"
Health care	Disease; suffering; bad outcomes; death	Patients and their families	Efficient, effective, and compassionate care
Software	Unreliable programs; slow processing; blue screens of death; porous security	Consumers who are frustrated or hacked	Technology that works safely
Manufacturing	High cost; restricted markets; unfulfilled delivery promises; dangerous products	Those who pay too much for inferior goods or who are harmed by them	Efficiencies and fairness
College Education	High tuition: degrees that don't lead to helpful employment; irrelevance	Students who graduate with a stack of debt and no job prospect	Affordable education providing marketable skills
	Poisonous chemicals	Anyone who breathes the air or drinks the water	Organic products that help plants grow without polluting[1]

Building stories around a brand helps the audience remain connected with it. For example, Maersk is a Danish transport and logistics giant company (I wrote about the company in Chapter 8.6). Its Instagram page has over 236,000 followers, dedicated to the staff's pictures and videos of shipping vessels and shipping containers. Shipping containers! Yes! Strangely enough, yes! Its community is highly engaged, and not only on Instagram. It has millions of fans on its Facebook page, several highly active LinkedIn groups that debate industry trends and several other social media channels to connect with its niche audience.

Figure 10-1 https://www.instagram.com/maersk_official/?hl=en

In his book "Building a StoryBrand," Donald Miller mentioned a remarkable story about the evolution of Apple towards becoming a consumer-centric innovative brand.

In 1983, Apple launched their computer Lisa with a nine-page ad in the New York Times, showed its technical features. When Steve Jobs returned to Apple after running Pixar, the animation movie company, Apple became customer-centric, compelling, and transparent in their communication. The first campaign Jobs published was nine pages in the New York Times. In 2007, the campaign message flipped 180 degrees to just two words on billboards all over America: "Think Different". When Apple started changing its communication to make it relevant and straightforward, it stopped featuring computers in most of its advertising. The customer is the hero in Apples' story; Customers do not buy the best products; they buy the products they can easily and quickly understand. Apple has inserted itself into their customers' story like no other technology company, and as a result, they are in the top ten most significant tech companies in 2021.[2]

In 2015, during the Sugar Bowl on New Year's Day, Allstate, the Insurance company, and the advertising agency Leo Burnett launched a campaign highlighting the risks of over-sharing location sign-in posts on social media. The story aimed to make people aware that sharing their whereabouts on social media might tip off criminals when burglarizing their homes. Allstate found a real couple to announce the project and led them to believe they had won a prize. First, they visited the couple in their home, secretly taking pictures of their household items and duplicating their belongings. Next, they invited the couple to attend the Sugar Bowl and were given their private box. Then, Mayhemsale.com began auctioning off the couple's belongings on national television during the game. People were directed to Mayhemsale.com for bargain-basement prices on everything the couples used. As the couple watched their possessions being sold on the big screens at the game, they panicked. Hidden cameras caught their reactions and broadcast them on live television. Of course, the couple's actual possessions were safe. The campaign agitated a fear in many Americans. U.S. News outlets, including ABC News, Wall Street Journal, and the New York Times, covered the story. Suddenly, the threat of criminals walking into homes as people announce distant whereabouts on social media became a U.S. national fear. The happy ending of a story was that Mayhemsale.com received 6,000 to 10,000 hits per second immediately following each commercial. The site received over 18 million hits during the game. Also, #Mayhemsale trended in the top ten hashtags during the game, and immediately after the commercials aired, surged to number one worldwide. Mayhem's Twitter followers increased by 24,000 during the game, and the first commercial of the campaign resulted in over 20 million impressions on Facebook and almost 70,000 likes. Allstate had foreshadowed a potential failure for their customers during one football game. It sold insurance, protecting them, opening a story loop, and offering to close it in a single campaign https://bit.ly/3unYQBp, https://bit.ly/3nMwwGp. 3

Figure 10-2 https://abcnews.go.com/WNT/video/allstate-commercial-highlights-risks-sharing-social-media-27983264

10.3 STORYTELLING CONCEPTS FOR A BRAND

1. Likewise, in their "Every seat, Southwest Airlines has a story." Create stories around the customer using the brand.
2. A story behind the scenes of making a brand. Loyal customers love a "sneak peek."
3. A story about the process used to create or develop a product: people love inspiration.
4. Tell the stories of staff and employees to emphasize a corporate culture and values.
5. Tell the story about why a brand was created and for what purpose.
6. A story about brands' values, 66% of the audience want the brands to stand up for social causes.[4]
7. A brand story that helped a customer to change their lives for better.
8. Create a story about how a brand is disrupting the business environment for better consumer advantage.
9. A brand is fighting the monopoly of other competitors who would not change their direction.
10. A story about a conflict that a brand resolved.
11. A story about dedicated employees, their motivation, and their passion for working for the brand.

On their website, Ace hardware states that they believe everyone has a story to tell. If you go through their website and social media accounts, you will be amazed at how many stories they tell around their brand, loyal consumers, and employees. They ask everyone interested to submit a story using the hashtag #HeartwareStories.

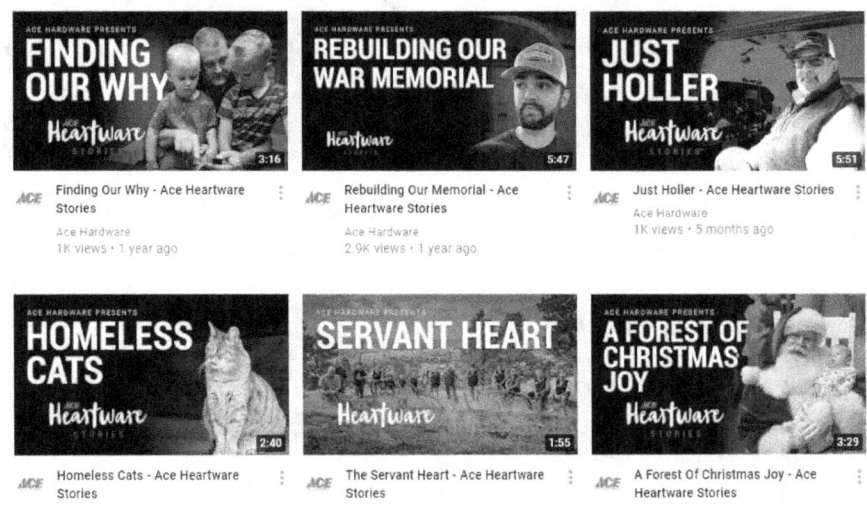

Figure 10-3 https://www.youtube.com/hashtag/heartwarestories

One of the remarkable stories they posted about their longest working employee, Wally, from Miner's Ace in California. Wally has been working at the company since 1958. The ninety-year-old Wally appeared in a YouTube video to discuss why he comes back to work each day for

over 60 years. The story gives a sentiment of high emotions and dedication of a loyal employee who has a passion for both his job and employer, which is exceedingly rare in our current days. Click these links to watch the full story, https://bit.ly/33gflUc, https://bit.ly/3nQQ8cl

Figure 10-4
https://www.facebook.com/acehardware/photos/a.268278017574/10157421433877575

10.4 REFERENCES

1. Stone, G., (2018) *Branding with Powerful Stories: The Villains, Victims, and Heroes Mode, Praeger.* https://amzn.to/3hu9Jwt
2. Fxssi (2021) *Top 10 World's Most Valuable Technology Companies in 2021,* https://bit.ly/3nSOjMk
3. Miller, D. (2017) *Building a StoryBrand: Clarify Your Message So Customers Will Listen, HarperCollins Leadership* https://amzn.to/2RLERhU.
4. Sprout Social (2017) *#BrandsGetReal: Championing change in the Age of social media,* https://bit.ly/3wVEUqv.

Chapter 11

11.1 A CORPORATE CORE STORY VS. BRAND STORY

A core story outlines the strategic direction and the purpose of the entire corporate brand. It acts as a compass directing all company communication, internally with its employees, investors, vendors, and externally, with its customers and the business environment. The more authentic and genuine stories promoted about the company values and purpose, the more the company will sustain its core story and identity. A corporate core storytelling goal is to anchor the company's values, visions, and culture. The next step is to explain these core values, deliver them through emotional stories, and communicate them to both internal and external audiences. Defiantly, the more impact will be through passionate storytelling.

Nike is a corporate core brand that exists independently of individual products. Nike Air is a subsidiary brand that supports the overall Nike corporate brand, emphasizing the soul of Nike and its core message. Procter & Gamble multi-brands like Pampers and Tide have solid self-stand product brands, and each individual has its own identity. At the same time, corporate Procter & Gamble stays silently in the background. The biggest challenge of the multi-brand corporation is to create individual brand identities and core stories that do not contradict each other and connect with the company's core corporate brand.

Figure 11-1 PROCTER & GAMBLE PAMPERS AND TIDE BRANDS

Nike's bold ad campaign "believe in something even it means sacrificing everything," starring Colin Kaepernick, the controversial former NFL quarterback, opened many arguments on social media. It is the first time Nike used conflict and controversial stories to establish their brand values. Nike is all about winning, no matter what. By delivering the sacrifice message, winning is about never quitting what someone believes. Nike used storytelling both internally and externally as a tool to enhance their heart-core message "To win." After the U.S. Women's National Soccer Team (USWNT) won its second consecutive World Cup, Nike aired a 60-second ad called "Never Stop Winning" to honor the victory. The ad focused on the idea that the win was more than another title but an essential step toward achieving pay equity and ending gender discrimination in sports.

11.2 BRAND STORY

If there is no story, it is just another commodity. A solid brand combines facts, functionality, culture, and emotions with the centric and the driving force. It is "who, what, and why" that a brand exists. A brand is the recognized added value and sentiments that a company or product represents by solving a problem or helping consumers feel comfort. Consumers' excellent perceptions of a brand convert them to the loyal tribe. A powerful brand represents a story that connects with the audience by transforming its identity into unique storylines to strengthen its purpose and proposition. For example, Spotify represents creativity and innovation as a default mindset. Spotify wants to unlock the potential of human creativity—by allowing a million creative artists to live off their art. Netflix represents "Streaming Ready." A convenience, affordability, and a range of films. For storytelling to become an effective tool for creating a brand concept, it shall reflect the brand values that can touch the consumer emotionally. In addition, these stories must have a consistent meaning.

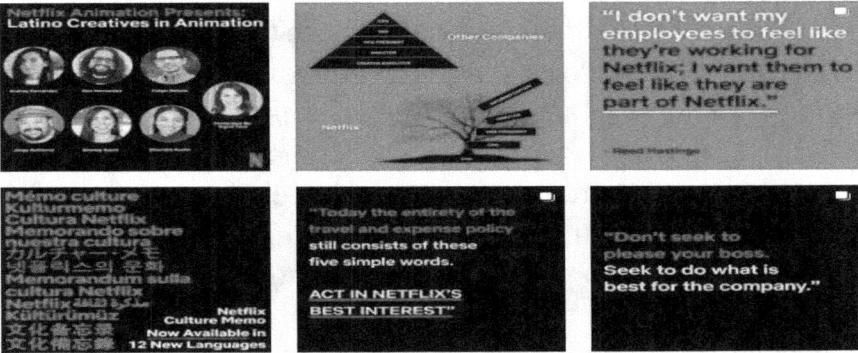

Figure 11-2 https://www.instagram.com/wearenetflix/

11.3 HOLISTIC APPROACH STORYTELLING

The most effective storytelling tool as a branding tool is to adopt a holistic approach and use the two techniques to build the central brand message. First, it communicates with the customers why a brand exists, what it stands for, who the buyers' persona is, why a brand is needed, and how customers can connect. A core story represents the heart and soul of a company. Second, it builds the bridge for the company's internal and external communication. In the business world, the adversary can act in any form. It could be the competitors or the companies themselves who do not innovate for a reason or do not have reliable customer service. Using storytelling elements helps a company create a sort of exciting internal challenge, or an "adversary," that employees should overcome through teamwork by applying a developed unique solution, skills, or some "heroism." [1]

A customer is a hero seeking to achieve a goal. The personalization of a hero character adds heart and soul to the company's role in the story world. It sheds light on the conflict and the passion that runs the brand forward. A brand must have a driving passion force for making a customer's life more positive. The supporting role is the product or service that helps the customer accomplish their dream. Thus, the customers are beneficiaries of the company's efforts to achieve its goal. A challenge is a villain that helps to unite the internal and external team players to confront it. It reinforces brands' spirit and culture while sending a coherent and bold message of their cultures and values to their broader surroundings. The core story aims to assemble a consistent structure of a company brand both internally and externally. If a company or brand does not stand for something other than making money, it will not make remarkable experiences for employees or customers or have a remembered emotional impact. The challenge is to summarize the company's core story in one sentence and deliver it to the world.

11.4 3M'S 15% CULTURE OF INNOVATION AND SUSTAINABILITY

3M is committed to sustainability and improving every life. For over 70 years, 3M's unique 15% culture has encouraged employees to set aside a portion of their work time to develop and engage in innovative ideas that motivate them proactively, https://bit.ly/3hqUrKa. The 3M 15% Culture gives employees the license to innovate. [2] It empowers every employee to develop visions, allowing all employees to spend 15% of their time on personal experiments and projects. In 3M, storytelling is an integrated part of the culture. Stories help employees understand what the company stands for through stories and ideas that encourage a culture of innovation. One unique idea may bring an invention to the world, like sandpapers or sticky notes. The story behind the invention of 3M's classic post-it note is written in several management books as an example of how a company thrives through a culture of innovation. 3M's core story is about purpose, according to Mike Roman, 3M CEO (2021). The company believes that "innovation isn't innovation without sustainability." For example, 3M innovates to reduce plastic use, improve environmental footprint. In addition, 3M commits to achieving carbon neutrality, minimizing water use, and enhancing water quality. The adversaries in these stories are all the things that stand in the way of ecosystems thrive, innovative thinking for purpose, diversified communities, and sustainability. 3 "How can we make sponges greener?" https://bit.ly/2RJkYYv is a 3M story told by curious kids about solutions to global challenges.

Figure 11-3
https://www.facebook.com/3MSingapore/photos/a.211145942235741/2785464014803908/

11.5 REFERENCES

1. Fog, K., Budtz, C., Munch, P., Blanchette, B., (2010). *Storytelling Branding in Practice.* Springer; 2nd Edition, pp 132, https://amzn.to/3vm3LCu
2. 3M (2021) *Core Elements to 3M's culture,* https://bit.ly/2SGWyjj
3. 3M (2021) *Sustainability,* https://bit.ly/2SGWpfL

Chapter 12

12.1 THE SIGNIFICANT ROLE OF CEOS IN THE BRAND STORYTELLING

CEOs' Stories are essential in the branding process. The CEO is a symbolic figure for any company besides his managerial and leadership duties. The CEOs must be more cautious and aware of their role in enlightening their company's brand and core values. CEOs' actions and speeches direct the path that the company is following. A CEO can destroy a company or brand by a very tiny mistake or be the icon of its success.

General Electric's former CEO, Jack Welch, who passed away in 2020, is famous for his candid, talent-centric management style and has long talked that companies are only as strong as those who keep them running. "Welch estimated he devoted about 60% of his time to human resources. This entire game of business revolves around one thing," he said at New York's World Business Forum. "You build the best team; you win." "You want your employees to feel like they are part of the company," Welch said. "Tell them a story that makes them want to choose you." [1]Many considered Jack Welch as the most outstanding leader of his era. As CEO of General Electric from 1981 to 2001, he transformed it from a company known for appliances and lightbulbs to a multinational corporation that stretched into financial services and media and industrial products. Under his leadership, G.E.'s company value soared by 4000%. When he retired from G.E., he received a severance payment of $417 million, the largest such payment in business history. 2

Figure 12-1 https://finance.yahoo.com

Elon Musk, CEO of Tesla Motors, is famous for innovative products and solutions. Musk, a South African-born American entrepreneur, and businessman founded X.com in 1999 (which later became PayPal), SpaceX in 2002, and Tesla Motors in 2003. Musk made headlines in May 2012, when SpaceX launched a rocket to send the first commercial vehicle to the International Space Station. Musk is working to transform transportation on Earth, electric car maker Tesla, and space via rocket producer SpaceX. Musk becomes a brand himself and an icon for innovation and recently becomes a source for pushing cryptocurrency and the stock market. For example, musk was behind GameStop's epic surge in Jan. 2021, tweeted out a link to the Reddit board that is largely hyped the stock.

Shares of GameStop were up over 60% in after-hours trading following Musk's tweet, linked to the "wallstreetbets" Reddit page with over 2 million subscribers.3 He has an enormous influence over his 57.7 million followers on Twitter, using his charming influence to promote many ideas and theories.

Figure 12-2 https://twitter.com/elonmusk

The CEO performs the lead role in stories, both internally and externally, in many successful brands. They become the StoryDriver of the company's core story. It occurs in companies where visionary and charismatic founders manage themselves. All a company's and CEOs' stories must aim in the same direction to enhance the company's one core story. It is a prerequisite for creating a consistent brand that can penetrate a highly competitive and crowded market.4

Gerald Ratner was the CEO of his family's jewelry business, Ratner Group. The company was struggling upon his arrival when he inherited it from his father in 1984. He transformed the company into a phase of prosperity and rapid expansion through his rebranding and cost-cutting. They were a low-price competitor, owned more than a thousand stores throughout Europe and the United States, 50% of the U.K. market. The road to ruin began in April 1991. Ratner was invited to speak at the Institute of Directors' meeting. It was a prestigious event attended by thousands of the U.K.'s most influential investors and covered by media and journalists. He made a joke about one of his company products in his speech, "People say, how can you sell this for such a low price? I say Because it's total crap." Then he also said, "We sold a pair of earrings for under a pound, which is cheaper than a shrimp sandwich from Marks and Spencer, but probably wouldn't last as long" https://bit.ly/3tJuEzz. 5

Figure 12-3 https://www.thegentlemansjournal.com/article/it-was-the-biggest-corporate-gaffe-of-all-time-five-lessons-from-the-rise-fall-and-rise-of-gerald-ratner/

The newspaper and TV outlets took Ratner's words literally, which degraded his company brand. After the speech, the value of the Ratner group plummeted by around £500 million, which nearly resulted in the firm's collapse. Ratner has said in his defense that his remarks were not meant to be taken seriously, but the jokes backfired and destroyed the company. Today, Ratner's speech is still famous in the corporate world as an example of the value of branding and image over quality.[6]

12.2 REFERENCES

1. Recognitionsource (2012), *Jack Welch's Tips For Managing Employees,* https://bit.ly/3f7mCeA.
2. Wikipedia (2021), *Jack Welch,* https://bit.ly/3h7Hlvv
3. CNBC (2021) *GameStop jumps after hours as Elon Musk tweets out Reddit board that is hyping stock,* https://cnb.cx/365wQrV
4. Fog, K., Budtz, C., Munch, P., Blanchette, B., (2010). *Storytelling Branding in Practice.* Springer; 2nd Edition, https://amzn.to/3vm3LCu
5. Kernan, S. (2020, September 23) *How a CEO Blew $10B With Three Bad Jokes,* https://bit.ly/2SPibxH
6. Wikipedia (2021), Gerald Ratner, https://bit.ly/3y4nklx

Chapter 13

13.1 GAPS IN STORYTELLING

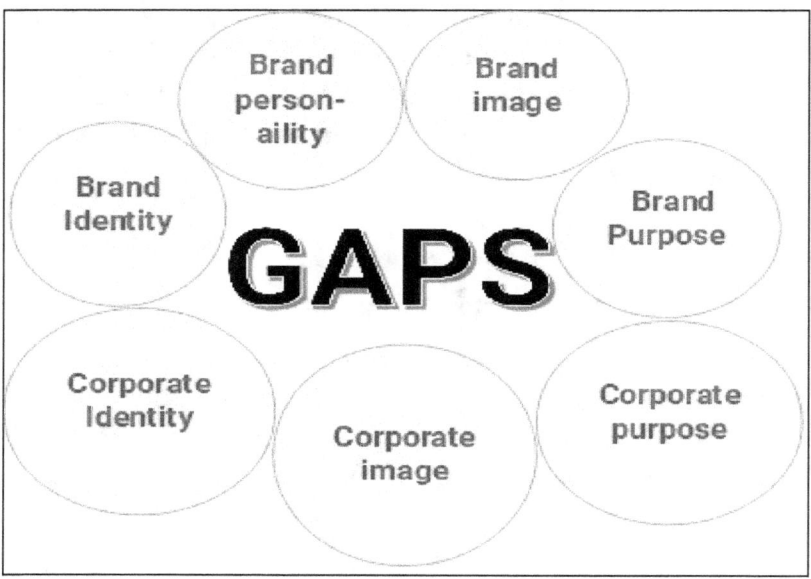

Figure 13-1 Gaps in storytelling

For developing a corporate core story that brands can revolve around in harmony, it is essential to know the nature of a likely gap between brand and corporate identity, image, and purpose. Some companies may experience a customer perception gap for several reasons. It could be a sort of definition or a communication problem. Without a proper explanation of brands' identity, image, and purpose, gaps will insufficiently influence and degrade marketing messages. Therefore, marketers shall define the gaps elements to fill them with non-contradicted and integrated storytelling messages. Sequentially, these consistent stories shall be communicated to the audience adequately to explain what it stands for.

Brand Identity	Brand Personality	Brand Image	Brand Purpose
A promise a company makes to a customer	Attitudes, emotions & characteristic	Customer perception of a brand A result of awareness & attractiveness for a brand	Product-led initiatives which strive to achieve business and society benefit simultaneously
Involves brand's name, colors, and logo to reflect brand's vision and message	Build personal relationships with consumers	Build upon customer interactions with a brand	Why a brand exists?
The brand fully controls the brand identity	Set of personal characteristics that are assigned to a brand	The brand has less control over the brand image	Brand's reason for being beyond making money

Figure 13-2 Brand identity, personality, image, and purpose comparison

The (Edelman 2017) study found that 50% of consumers worldwide consider themselves belief-driven buyers, and 67% bought a brand for the first time because they agreed with its position on a controversial topic. The result concludes that a powerful brand purpose can set a company apart from the crowd. (The Edelman 2020) Trust barometer special report revealed that 74% of a brand's impact on society is why brand trust has become more important; 64% said that trust is second to price, making brands' trust the make-or-break difference.[1] The dynamics of a powerful brand exist precisely because the brand is constantly fighting to overcome challenges and adversaries to achieve its goal. A "purpose" does not necessarily mean that the brand must pursue an ideological quest. However, it means that brands need to position and differentiate themselves in the business and support societies and communities with a worthwhile cause. For instance, Black Lives Matter created a social reason for brands to talk about and interact with audiences to gain trust. Consumers are looking to brands to act and advocate for change in a systemic racism environment.[2]

13.2 WARBY PARKER BRAND'S PERSONALITY

A marvelous story shows the brand's personality, solution, and social commitment. Warby Parker is a lifestyle brand eyewear company that offers designer eyewear at a revolutionary price. Brands' story "to offer designer eyewear at a revolutionary price while leading the way for social businesses." The company wants to fight market monopoly and satisfy the customers with unique designs, higher quality, and affordable prices.

Brand's purpose is a commitment to benefit society. Its website story, "One billion people worldwide lack access to glasses." Warby Parker partners with non-profits like Vision Spring to make sure that for every pair of glasses sold, a pair is delivered to someone in need." [3] The brand existed because one of its founders lost a pair of glasses on a backpacking trip and waited an entire semester of graduate

school to replace them because of the prohibitive cost. This bad personal experience was the driving force behind the brand. The brand sympathizes with customers who have eyewear issues. Warby Parker is not just some startup with its eye on disruption; it is a company designed to serve a segment of the population that is being ignored. The company's compelling brand storytelling has paid off https://bit.ly/3elo7ks by a series of videos, social media posts, and by making a documentary showing the entire process of making Warby Parker glasses, from the initial design to cutting the lenses. They send a personalization message to the customer "When you order, a new pair is made just for you. "The brand is valued at $3 billion in 2021.
<u>4</u>

Figure 13-3 <u>https://www.instagram.com/warbyparker/?hl=en</u>

13.3 REFERENCES

1. Edelman (2017) *Earned-brand-2017,* https://bit.ly/367l4Nt
2. Edelman (2020), *Brand-trust-2020,* https://bit.ly/366IIcS
3. Warby Parker (2021) https://www.warbyparker.com/history
4. Roof, K., Baker, L., (2021, April 21) *Warby Parker is considering an IPO,* https://bit.ly/36cTuOM

Chapter 14

14.1 STORYTELLING IN ADVERTISING

Ace Metrix measures the performance and strength of emotional connection in storytelling advertising. The released report "2019's Best Storytelling Ads" revealed that outstanding storytelling alone does not make an effective ad. With over 8,400 video ads analyzed in 2019 and over 3 million viewer comments, the top 10 ads distinguished themselves by telling real-life stories, historical tales, and inspirational acts. While they differ in their delivery, they all cause a magnitude of emotions in viewers. The top ten ads in 2019 Best Storytelling Ads are emotions that fire. [1]

Mercedes's "Bertha Benz" https://bit.ly/3uW6Fyw ranked the top storytelling ad with the highest emotional connection, powerful messaging, inspiring, and heartfelt feelings. The respondent comments phrases like "love the storyline," measured and analyzed by natural language machine learning. "Dramatic story," "powerful history," and "tells a Powerful Storytelling ads create long-lasting emotional bonds with customers, which help the brands remain attached to customers' subconscious memory. In addition, a story is necessary to become the driving force behind its brand values, differentiating them in very crowded, noisy media outlets. Therefore, companies need to re-evaluate and analyze the performance of their ads to understand brands' reception and consumers' behaviors. A consistent strategy is crucial for ads to reflect core stories, values, and promises to avoid contradictory messages. Consistency will help the customers understand brands' identity, personality, image, and purpose and encourage engagement involves two-way communication. Ads shall be tailored and personalized according to the buyer persona, not based on an un-relevant audience. Consistency enhances brand confidence and trust, an essential trigger for customer purchasing decisions second to price. Stories should be enjoyable and engaging with their niche customer audience, reflecting their real-life stories, concerns, struggles, conflicts, and challenges. The customers shall play the hero role in the conflict's story plot of escalating events pursuing their ambitious goals. A brand shall play a supporting and guiding role in the hero's journey. The emotional meaning of the story is a prominent part of a successful ad encouraging the customers to connect, respond and interact with the brand message.

14.2 TRAVELERS REAL-LIFE STORY ADS " THE TREEHOUSE: HOWARD'S UNFINISHED STORY"

Travelers is an insurance company in the United States. The company used storytelling techniques ads to promote their services. They interviewed some relatives of accident victims to talk about their beloved real-life ones who are lost in an accident. Travelers continued to tell an unfinished story about an accident victim, which triggers emotional connections and empathy among the viewers. They presented the victim as the hero of the story while the company solutions sit in the backseat.

This ad https://bit.ly/3oovwbY is about Howard's who was a self-taught grandfather carpenter. A distracted driver killed him while he pulled over to the side of the road. Travelers wanted the audience to be aware of car accidents caused by distracted drivers that can be avoided. In the video description, "Each day, nine people are killed by distracted driving, leaving their stories unfinished. We honored Howard by bringing his Unfinished Story to life by imagining what could have been". Travelers transformed this valuable awareness message into emotional storytelling to promote their service cleverly and indirectly.

Figure 14-1 The Treehouse: Howard's Unfinished Story

14.3 NESCAFÉ GOLD BLEND LOVE STORY

In 1987, Nestle launched its campaign for NESCAFE Gold Blend in the U.K. The series of ads were about a suspense romantic love story https://bit.ly/3yguweb. The ads told the story of Tony and Sharon, two opposites who slowly attract, thanks to their shared love of Gold Blend coffee. The campaign ran in the U.K. from 1987 to 1993. The Nescafe brand was not the hero in the story, but it was why the two lovers meet each other for the first time simply because they love drinking coffee, and it was a Nescafe brand. Usually, humans love to interact with other humans who share the same taste, traditions, values, culture, religion, or language. It was the core story of Nescafe that lasted for several years. It was a story about good taste and passion, an entertaining story that got viewers' attention: the focus was on the characters and their actions while NESCAFE took a supporting role in the back seat. However, it still managed to play an essential role in developing the story. More importantly, since 1987, NESCAFE Gold Blend has increased its sales by 60%. 2 When the Gold Blend campaign was running, there used to be newspaper ads that advertised when the next installment would be on TV. The campaign did a great job of building anticipation. Marketers could do similar stories with the power of social media, inviting the audience to develop brand storytelling and use social media hashtags to build excitement for each episode. This kind of ad campaign would undoubtedly prompt many conversations around a brand and extend its exposure.

Figure 14-2 Nescafé Gold Blend - After These Messages

14.4 DISCOVER YOUR WINGS – UNIVERSITY OF PHOENIX

"As a working adult, it's normal to feel like you're too busy to earn your degree" https://bit.ly/3ydMDS8. It is an ad story about a mother struggling to raise her kid. She wants a better future, a more secure and paying job; therefore, when she saw an ad for a part-time business degree by the University of Phoenix, she dreamed of flying into a better future. The university commercial is sending a message to busy people with the ambition that it will help them reach their potential goal. "It's time to see how far your wings can take you." The emotional narrative built a strong connection with viewers, especially with people who may have the same living conditions as the heroes' story. The comments and the viewers' interactions are also emotional; the audience sympathizes with the struggling mother. One more time, the brand did not take a lead hero role in the story and remained in the back seat to support the hero in her journey pursuing her goal.

Figure 14-3 Discover Your Wings–University of Phoenix

14.5 REFERENCES

1. Ace Metrix (2020) *The Best Storytelling Ads in 2019*, https://bit.ly/33JVj4P
2. Fog, K., Budtz, C., Munch, P., Blanchette, B., (2010). *Storytelling Branding in Practice. Springer*; 2nd Edition Page 166, https://amzn.to/3vm3LCu

Chapter 15

Storytelling Is a Powerful Communication Tool

"Storytelling is the art of communication using stories and narratives"

15.1 BRAND COMMUNICATION

Consumer skepticism has always been a problem for brands; therefore, brands need to be trusted, authentic, and effective in communication. The (Edelman 2019) Trust Barometer Special Report: In Brands, We Trust? An eight-country study showed that 81% of consumers across markets, ages, incomes, and gender say that brand trust is essential to buying. [1] Brand communication is a direct interaction between a brand and its internal and external stakeholders. It is a combination of TV or radio or online advertising, social media, reviews, emails, online or paper newsletters, and billboards used to communicate internally and externally. Consistency is crucial between all channels, which requires using unified and noncontradiction messages. Brand visuals such as colors, logos, tags, symbols all must be consistent. (McKinsey & Company 2017) revealed that only 13% of customers remained loyal to a brand in 2017. 87% considered other brands while 58% switched to a new one. [2]

The switch off from one brand to another is evidence of poor communication in some respects. There might be other reasons related to the brand itself for not adding value or solving customer problems. For instance, the evolution of mobile shopping apps that showcase options, simplify pricing, compare product specifications, and facilitate peer reviews make it possible to size up brands effortlessly. In addition, social media lets consumers know what their friends are buying and what they like and dislike about those purchases. All this encourages consumers to shop around and changes patterns that marketers have counted on for years. In contrast, the primary goal of marketing communication is to reach a clearly defined audience and influence its purchasing behavior by building awareness and stimulating customer trials. On the other hand, brand communication is successful if it creates the desired response in that audience. The goal is to keep consumers connected with the brand and enhance customer loyalty. Brands need to improve products and services and make them more valuable for the consumers. Apple has outgrown competitors by offering differentiated product innovation and a better consumer experience. During the recession that occurred in 2008, Hyundai did not follow the usual car industry playbook by stopping the bleeding with short-term sales incentives. Instead, the company used an innovative marketing campaign to build consideration. It promised to take back cars from customers who had lost their jobs or incomes to drive up consideration among consumers financially unsettled by the recession. Further, Hyundai was one of the very few auto companies to grow when the industry was widely losing ground at that time, https://bit.ly/3fTCrWB.

Following are some routes of brand communication: -

1) Leadership Communication

The decision-makers at the top of the pyramid need to be at the heart of the branding process. The leader will be ultimately responsible for crafting the messaging proposition, defining the brand direction, and cascading this message to their teams. For example, in a recent video, "Cars Moment: Recharge," Håkan Samuelsson, Chief Executive Volvo cars, announced Volvo's new strategy "Sustainability is now as important as safety to us." The purpose is to influence the necessary change to motivate stakeholders and create a buy into a strategy https://bit.ly/3fOrdCM.

2) Change Communication

In a business life cycle, companies may face several difficulties. For example, there might be structural changes or mergers and acquisitions or simply economic drawdown periods or disruptive technologies, pandemic such as covid - 2019 where jobs must be eliminated and staff to be laid off. Communicating these changes in emotional storytelling to the stakeholders can help to increase the trust and the transparency of the brand.

3) Sharing The Company's Mission, Vision, And Culture

Lego had created an animated video to celebrate its 80th anniversary. Through the art of storytelling, Lego beautifully communicated how it started its business, combating struggles and ups and downs and how its culture and values were shaped over the years https://bit.ly/2SsCocp.

4) Learning And Development

Storytelling techniques can share personal experiences, technical frameworks, technologies, and models to help learners understand the practical application of knowledge.

5) Coaching And Learning

Coaching techniques are better delivered to the audience through a life story. Coaches take the learners through their journey, ups and downs, and turning points. It helps the learners connect with their coach, and it also keeps the coaching authentic and not a hypothetical journey. 3

6) Customers' Testimonials

With a visual story context, customers' testimonials are more exciting and far more memorable and impactful. Customer testimonials stories demonstrate a customer's need, show how the company or brand fills that need, and improve the customer's life by using brands' services or products. Tesla successfully did this by posting a series of customer stories, a mix of <u>video testimonials</u> and stories spoken by the Teslas' customers themselves. These stories show real Tesla customers interacting with their cars and how being a Tesla owner has improved the customer's life positively.

Figure 15-1 https://www.tesla.com/customer-stories

7) Employees' Testimonials

Employees are a fundamental element that shapes the company's core values and culture. Marketers can use storytelling to showcase employees' achievements and assign them ambassadors for the brand. The types of people the company employs, and the things they are passionate about, communicate massively about the company's values and culture. Employees' stories help communicate that culture to audiences who will connect with employee stories on an emotional & personal level. The environmentally friendly clothing company Reformation showcases short employee story videos on Instagram and YouTube. The videos https://bit.ly/2QLMp3J feature Reformation employees are working in the factory where the clothes are produced. The **video series** showing the factory employees telling their life stories and daily routines is a solid storytelling approach.

Figure 15-2 https://www.thereformation.com/pages/sustainability-report-q1-2021

8) Brand Influencer Communication

According to (Takumi 2020) research, "the covid climate has led their clients to lean more heavily into influencers. From a cultural perspective, with social media consumption up significantly, influencers are more influential than ever."[4] Data from the (MuseFind 2018) report showed that 92% of consumers trusted an influencer more than an advertisement or traditional celebrity endorsement. A study by (gen. video 2017) found that 33% said influencers were trusted sources when making shopping decisions, while only 17% trusted friends and family for shopping recommendations. Influencers provided insight into their personal lives and interacted with their followers. By responding to messages, giving their opinions influencers are more impactful to followers than their celebrity counterparts. [5]

(Takumi 2020) research revealed that people most trusted YouTube content creators. Influencer marketing is estimated to be worth $15 billion by 2022, almost double its value in 2019 -$8 billion-. 27% of 16-44-year-olds were influenced to buy a service or product by YouTube influencers during the past six months of collecting the data. In contrast, 24% were influenced by Instagram creators and 15% by TikTok creators. Furthermore, younger consumers (16-24-year-olds) are more likely to buy a product or service due to TikTok influencers as 30% in the United Kingdom and 40% in Germany were influenced to purchase a product or service by TikTok influencers. In comparison, 37% of 33-44-year-olds were most influenced by TikTok influencers in the United States.

Meanwhile, 38% of 25-34-year-olds in the U.K. and 59% of 25-34-year-olds in Germany were influenced to purchase by YouTube and Instagram influencers, compared to the U.S., where 57% of 35-44-year-olds were influenced by Instagram and YouTube content creators. The research showed that consumers trusted influencers more than they trust the information coming from a brand. Now more than ever, a brand message is competing with traditional media, word-of-mouth, online reviews, blogs, and more. Brands that can educate and entertain their audiences via influencers will capture consumers' hearts and wallets compared to traditional media. However, marketers' trust in different channels differs, with Instagram being ranked on top, followed by YouTube and TikTok. One of the top three concerns for marketers included a 'lack of familiarity with TikTok, while 96% of marketers felt familiar with Google's

YouTube. With that being said, the ability of creators to demonstrate return on investment could enhance the trust of marketers. The report also states that customers recognized Instagram as more aspirational, informational, and easy to use than TikTok. 6 In contrast, consumers consider TikTok more engaging and creative than Instagram.

To leverage influencers for brand storytelling content for maximum impact, brands must learn how to:
- Discover the right influencers and sign them up.
- Measure the success of influencers.
- Brand storytelling needs a storyteller. Some of the most compelling storytellers are influencers. The best ones already love the brand; they can be found through social listening or agencies. The high-quality content creators that already used brand hashtags and talked about the products on social media are the best choice to leverage communication and emotional reactions.

15.2 BRAND AUTHENTIC AND CONSISTENT COMMUNICATION MESSAGES

Consumers respond to authenticity. Storytelling allows to bring personality and authenticity to brand marketing messages, and it is a powerful tool for delivering what consumers desire. Brand communication requires consistency across multiple mediums and social media channels. Consistency is a crucial deliverable because it promotes its by including storytelling in their brand communication strategies, companies can provide platforms for spreading stories about their consumers and building brand loyalty. In addition, well-told and communicated stories prompt ongoing conversations and generate followings and patronage.

15.3 THE PURPOSE LAW

The ultimate reason for every company is the purpose for its existence. Brand purpose is the reason that business exists beyond making money. Of course, not every company has a solid basis for its existence beyond making profits. Nowadays, many companies and big brands try to show their purpose to become more recognized in the noisy, crowded marketplace. Big brands such as Dove, the Bodyshop, Unilever Apple, Ikea, Ted, and many others created social media campaigns to deliver their purpose messages in the shape of storytelling https://bit.ly/3iap1bJ, https://bit.ly/2SfPslo. Unilever stated that its purpose-led brands grow 69% faster than the rest of their business. It is a clear signal that brands with sustainability at their core are beneficial to both people and the planet. Here are some examples of brand purpose inspirations: -

TED "Ideas Worth Spreading"
Dove "Help women everywhere develop a positive relationship with the way they look, helping them realize their full potential"
TESLA" To Accelerate the world transition to sustainable energy"
PATAGONIA "We're in business to save our home planet"

When the purpose is identified, communicating brands' identity becomes more straightforward and incredibly powerful. It provides customers, partners, vendors, and employees possibilities to feel like they are a part of a brands' tribe. A brand's purpose provides a sense of belonging and togetherness, initiating a movement to build up around its purpose. The purpose should be the core, the soul, of a business. Every action of that business should authentically convey its purpose and meaning. If employees can recognize the company's core story, they will proudly share it. A strong brand always starts internally to enhance its purpose message with its employees to have a long-term effect externally. If Nike's employees could not identify and advocate their belief in "the will to win," sooner before later, the prestigious brand commercials will seem silly and forgettable. Employees are the single key ambassadors of a company brand. 7

15.4 COMMUNICATING THE PURPOSE AND THE COMPANY'S CULTURE

15.4.1.1   Burger King, "Whopper free zone"

In 2007, Burger King carried out a social experiment to remind the Americans' love of the Whopper visible. First, they declared a random Burger King restaurant a "Whopper free zone." Then, they temporarily took the Whopper off the menu to measure consumers' reactions. Naturally, the consumers were unhappy, and many were annoyed and complained about the unavailable beloved burger https://bit.ly/3hJR4yp, https://bit.ly/2T4dsYQ. The campaign affected Burger King restaurants' sales, with Whopper quarterly sales increase up by double digits.

The ad campaign was awarded a Gold Effie in the restaurant's category, the top award given to acknowledge effectiveness for the campaign's "boldness and creativity across multiple media platforms." Moreover, fewer customers visited the competing burger restaurants. Burger King proved the Whopper is much more than just a burger; it is a part of American culture. 8

Figure 15-3 Burger King Shocks Customers: NO MORE WHOPPERS!

15.4.1.2 Dollar Shave Club

In 2011, Michael Dubin met a friend's father-in-law at a party who had a warehouse filled with razor blades he wanted to sell. The concept for Dollar Shave Club is about building a passionate tribe around a feasible demand. The idea behind the business is to compete against those dominant brands such as Gillet, which offers high prices for its several blades razor packages. While Dollar shave club provides low prices, it builds up a community movement around itself. Establishing a social movement community would make it more appealing for customers who want to fight big dominant brands. The rise of social media apps helped spread the newborn brand.

Michael Dubin had a brilliant idea about a promotion video that stars Michael himself walking through a warehouse while talking about the company's purpose. The video generated over 12,000 orders on that day and has since been viewed over 27 million times https://bit.ly/2Slosk8.But, while one viral video makes for a splendid start, Dollar Shave Club knew it could not stop there. If the company was genuinely going to improve the customer experience in purchasing razors, Michael knew it needed to do more than sell. So, inspired by the notion of a member's club, Michael branded himself the "Club Pro," a confidently trusted mentor who would answer all the weird and wonderful questions his customers could dream up. The company then decided to lead the conversation with helpful, humorous, socialized engaging content.

Figure 15-4 Dollar shave club viral YouTube video

Dollar Shave Club's core belief and purpose have not changed since its inception. Even though business strategies change and grow, the core purpose stays consistent. For example, Ford's purpose is to "open the highways to all mankind", Southwest Airline's purpose of providing affordable transportation to the common person; Walt Disney's purpose is to bring joy to children everywhere, and Coca-Cola's purpose is to inspire happiness. Serving its purpose, Dollar Shave Club went from a one-person operation to a mega brand. Unilever eventually acquired it for $1 billion. Dollar Shave Club's website or social media channels today still at the same spirit and purpose in everything that it does. A company's purpose will shape its brand's values, as well as its personality and voice.[7]

15.4.1.3 *Airbnb's #WeAccept campaign*

In 2017 Airbnb launched a campaign on short notice in response to President Donald Trump's travel ban and starred its employees. The camera zooms in on the diverse faces of Airbnb's employees as the audience read titles, "We believe no matter who you are, where you're from, whom you love, or whom you worship, we all belong. The world is more beautiful the more you accept #WeAccept." [9]

Given that the Super Bowl was just days away, the company took the opportunity and purchase a 30-second spot to run the video during the game for maximum awareness. In addition, the #WeAccept campaign included a letter from Airbnb's founders featured on its website, plus social media content featuring personal stories from its employees: https://www.airbnb.co.uk/weaccept. The letter states, "We know this is an idealistic notion that faces tremendous obstacles because of something that also seems simple but isn't—that not everyone is accepted. The letter then showcases Airbnb's goal of providing short-term housing to over 100,000 people refugees, disaster survivors, and relief workers over five years. Airbnb's stance, combined with the quality of its message and timing, resulted in #WeAccept becoming the most tweeted hashtag during Super Bowl, with over 33,000 tweets and 87 million earned impressions.

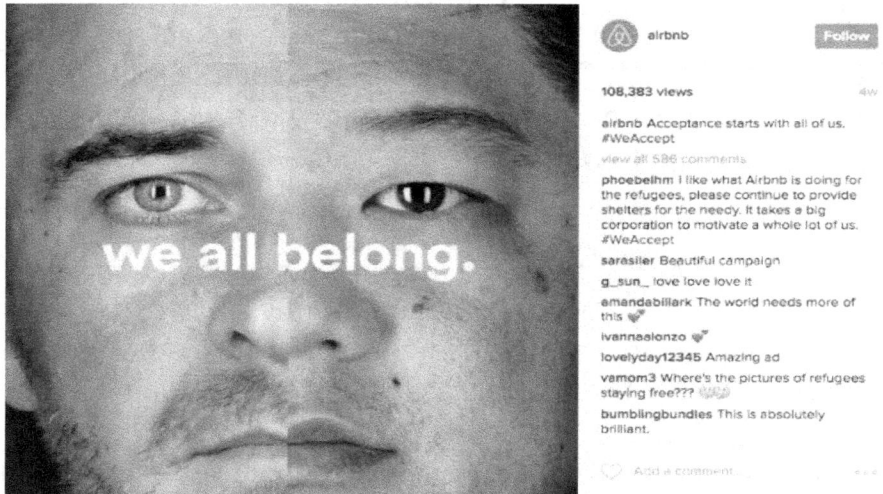

Figure 15-5 Airbnb takes a stand with #WeAccept

In addition, 60 global news outlets covered it, crediting Airbnb for not only making a bold statement but for creating a solid call to action for its community to join in and help. Airbnb continues to document its progress on its website, citing over 15,000 of its members volunteering to donate their homes and over $4 million raised for the International Rescue Committee. Furthermore, #WeAccept reinforces the

type of customer and community Airbnb has and will continue to build. Of course, when a company takes a stand, it will not appeal to everyone. However, if the brand deeply understands its core customer base and aligns its stance with significant issues, that is where the magic happens.

By acting on what it believed in, Airbnb made its existing customers proud and attracted a group of like-minded customers to join its tribe.

(Sprout social 2017) report "Championing Change in the Age of Social Media" uncovered that people would like brands to take a stance on social and political issues in social media. 66% felt that topics such as immigration, human rights, and race relations need to be addressed by brands. Relevance is key to reception. 47% of consumers say brands are most credible when an issue directly impacts their customers, while 40% see credibility on matters affecting employees and 30 % in business operations.[10]

15.5 Brand Communication in social media

People believe brands and social media can empower connections. 91% of people believe in social's power to connect people despite feelings of division. Further, 78% of consumers wanted brands to use social to help people connect. When customers feel connected to brands, more than half of consumers, 57%, will increase their spending with that brand, and 76% will buy from them over a competitor. Consumers wanted to learn more about the people behind their beloved brands. For instance, 70% of consumers feel more connected when a brand's CEO is active on social. 72% of consumers report feeling connected when employees share information about a brand online. According to sprout social research, 65% of consumers feel more connected to brands with a robust social presence. That means brands must focus on their content's consistency and quality.[11]

Notably, consumers want material that humanizes an otherwise faceless brand, and they wanted the people behind the brands doing the posting. The social behavior from highly engaged brands with customers enhances sales engagement. Answering a customer's question on social prompts sales. According to sprouts' (2017), 48% of customers purchase from a responsive brand on social media. Companies shall monitor mentions and conversations about brands' products ,hashtags , employees ,competitors ,and customers. Social listening helps track, analyze, and respond to discussions across the internet. Brands need to use hashtags to centralize conversation on social media so that their customer can find it and engage with it. 12

15.5.1.1 Former Papa John's CEO on the call that cost him his career

Former Papa John's CEO John Schnatter, during a call in 2018, used a racial word that led him to be removed from the company https://bit.ly/3fG1jRJ. The company hired an agency to help the brand re-build its image and identity and re-establish connections with its consumers through emotional storytelling and social transparency. They avoided launching an apology tour for Schnatter's word. Instead, the company created the "Voices of Papa John's " campaign, a series of short videos profiling the brand's diversified ethnic employees, explaining why they value working at Papa John's.

Figure 15-6 Former Papa John's CEO on the call that cost him his career

15.5.1.2 Yoplait, You've Got This, Mom On!

Imagine that an Australian yogurt brand wants to tackle a social issue about mothers to shine among its competitors as a genuine value brand. Yoplait aspired to send this message to its female customer mothers, "The first rule of motherhood, someone's always judging. So, to all the moms out there, we see you and say, Mom On!" https://bit.ly/3p17zI5 Yoplait tapped into a shared public debate: mum-shaming. It relates to the often preachy or patronizing information given to mothers about being a good parent and shaming those who do not follow it. In Its 2018 campaign, 'Mom On' depicted mothers addressing common criticisms they face, such as a judgment over breastfeeding, going back to work. While the ad did not focus on a current event or overly controversial subject, it presented the brand stance bold on a specific issue, with the clear potential to offend those who might disagree. The social stance made the campaign hugely memorable, standing out amid a sea of similar and formulaic ads from competitor brands. 9

Figure 15-7 Yoplait You've Got This, Mom On!

15.5.1.3   Airbnb "Wall and Chain"

Catherine was an Airbnb guest in May 2012. She traveled to Berlin with her father, Jörg, a Berlin Wall guard at the Cold War. Catherine told Airbnb about an incident that made the trip a powerful story. She wanted to show her father the vibrant city of Berlin how it changed, but coincidence happened that it was the man they met at their rented Airbnb apartment that changed everything for Jörg. As a result, Airbnb connected two Berlin wall border guards back together. Airbnb felt that telling an inspirational story is the best way to connect and belong to each other, making them feel emotional and associated with the brand. The intelligent, fantastic, and cool animation, "Wall and Chain" https://bit.ly/3flqABD tied immediately into the international 'be anywhere' feel the company has worked hard to create.

Figure 15-8 Breaking Down Walls | Wall & Chain | Airbnb

The story at the heat of the animation is about a genuine and authentic story to let the customer buy in the core message and believe in it. Anyone who watches the animation will be impacted by the simplicity of the ideas at its heart. It is about connection, family, and being a global citizen. What made the captivating story more compelling is that it is delivered with such simple animation. The animation was told in an intense and instantly memorable story, as the emotions that pour out of it are phenomenal.

15.5.1.4 Buy My Barina, Barinageddon

David decided it was time to sell his beloved 1999 Barina car with 188,000+ kilometers on the odometer, only three hubcaps, and its share of dents and scratches. David, who worked for a video production company, had a brilliant idea with the help of his colleagues to let bring Barina to life in the most epic used car sales video ever. They came up with the clever tagline, "Don't just make history—drive it" https://bit.ly/2RQnnRF. He received valid offers of $1,000 and $2,000 (double the asking price). Finally, Australia's NRMA Insurance made David an offer he could not refuse. NRMA Insurance, a company that offers a range of automotive and home insurance solutions, wanted to buy the car. David accepted and donated the money to Cancer Council Australia.

The company wanted to use Barina's fame to tell a story about the work the NRMA Insurance research center carries out with physical testing, data analysis, consumer advisory on car safety, and comprehensive car insurance reduction https://bit.ly/3yGn0K8.

Figure 15-9 Tweet me an offer using the hashtag #buymybarina

It was a brilliant move for NRMA Insurance to jump onto the board of Barina's story. NRMA Insurance took Barina's success story and leveraged it to showcase the work it does in its R&D lab. When a brand industry is more formal, like an insurance company, telling a story in a fun, creative way differentiates it from its counterpart competitors. [7]

15.5.1.5   A hair-raising message

The Swedish Childhood Cancer Foundation wanted to make a bold ad that emotionally affects the people passing a subway train to help donate for children combating cancer diseases. So, just as the passenger arrives, a static billboard of a young woman with long hair comes to life, and her hair starts to blow around. It is as if the wind generated by the train's arrival is propelling the movement of her hair in real-time.

However, as the train slows down, the wind blowing the woman's hair exposes her bald head. A shocked expression likely replaces the passenger's surprise and smile. They are stunned, trying to figure out what just happened. The billboard's animation ends with the message "Every day a child is diagnosed with cancer" and invites you to text a specific number to donate to the foundation.

Figure 15-10 The Swedish Childhood Cancer Foundation, a hair-raising message

A video released by the nonprofit captured the powerful reactions to the billboard from people on the train platform, expressing their shock and sadness: https://bit.ly/3i0jzb5. The Sooner the video was shared across social networks and news media, the passionately it responded in Sweden and worldwide. The foundation's pioneering use of innovative technology in its visual storytelling successfully raised awareness and funds for childhood cancer. The right visuals appeal to human emotions and make a story memorable. Stories communicate values. But they also communicate knowledge. By exchanging stories, brands share knowledge. Stories information packaged in a meaningful context is more accessible for the audience to understand its depth and relevance. 7

15.5.1.6   Häagen-Dazs Passionate Story

Since 2008, the company has used its platform to talk about waning honeybee populations, telling stories to persuade their audience to action. It has been done through its Honeybees initiative. Honeybees pollinate one-third of the foods we eat, including many of the ingredients Häagen-Dazs used to make their pure ice creams, sorbets, frozen yogurts, and bars. Unfortunately, honeybee populations are disappearing at an alarming rate. So Häagen-Dazs ice cream has teamed up with leading research facilities to donate more than $1,000,000 to honeybee research. One of their most results methods of highlighting the honeybee's plight is the modern virtual reality methods: https://bit.ly/2SSj2Oq.

The educational VR video invites the viewer to fly along with a bee named Alex as he shows them the threats facing his species. Häagen-Dazs hopes that this award-winning video will help bring the plight of the bees the attention it deserves https://www.haagendazs.us/save-the-honey-bees.

Figure 15-11 Passionate-stories-haagen-dazs

15.6 BRAND COMMUNICATION THROUGH LOGOS AND COLORS

The psychology of color relates to persuasion aspects of marketing & branding. It helps to understand perception and consumer behaviors. Further, color helps humans memorize certain information by increasing their attentional level. The secretariat of the Seoul international color expo researched in 2004 revealed the following relationships between color and marketing:
92.6% said they put the most importance on visual factors when purchasing products. Only 5.6% said that the physical feel via the sense of touch was most important. Hearing and smell each drew 0.9%. 84.7% of the total respondents thought that color accounts for more than half of the various factors essential for choosing products. The University of Loyola, Maryland, performed a study that revealed that color increases brand recognition by 80%. The Midwestern U.S. insurance company used color to highlight essential

information on their invoices. Consequently, they began receiving customer payments an average of 14 days earlier. Customers remember documents and presentations better when color is used. 13

15.6.1.1 Heinz EZ Squirt Green Ketchup

Heinz introduced EZ Squirt ketchup for children in the early 2000s. The company introduced artificially colored ketchup that featured a nozzle like a glue bottle and allowed the user to squirt the colorful mixture on foods. The first color rolled out was green, followed by blue, purple, and a mystery color (kids love mystery colors), which could be orange, teal, or purple. From 2000 to 2003, the company sold over 25 million bottles of the condiment. However, like so many colorful fads, this one wore off as well, and the product was discontinued in 2006. As time went on, consumers have become more health-conscious, limiting, or banning artificial food dyes in some areas. While this may not have directly affected EZ Squirt, it was likely a factor in its waning popularity. 14

Colors express different emotions and personalities. Here are some popular colors and what they symbolize:
Yellow: optimism, clarity, warmth
Orange: friendly, cheerful, confident
Red: excitement, bold, youthful
Purple: creative, wise, imaginative
Blue: trust, strength, dependable
Green: peaceful, growth, health
Gray: balance, neutral, calm

Many brands whose products deal with the environment utilize green. John Deere, Animal Planet, and the Girl Scouts all use this color. Green's value goes beyond nature-focused companies. Food manufacturers take advantage of the fact that people associate green with health.

Gray plays an essential role in the logo world, especially when it is shined to a silver finish. Car companies like Mercedes-Benz and Honda use logos that feature silver. Some companies that are partial to red include Target, Coca-Cola, and Netflix. In contrast, iconic technology brands such as Dell, IBM, Intel, and G.E. leverage blue's robust and trustworthy persona to represent their brands. Whole Foods, Starbucks, and Girl Scouts use green to showcase a peaceful, healthful brand identity. 15

Table 15-12 Heinz EZ Squirt colored ketchup

15.7 REFERENCES

1. Edelman (2019) *Trust barometer special report: in brands we trust,* https://bit.ly/3fNScQc
2. Court, D., ElzingaD., Finneman, B., and Perrey, J., (2017, February 24), *The new battleground for marketing-led growth,* https://mck.co/3uyNzgM
3. Nandy, P. (2017, March 23), *How top companies use storytelling to drive results on,* https://bit.ly/3bP16dR
4. Takumi (2020) Into the mainstream, https://bit.ly/2TtC0uv
5. Questionpro (2021) *Why Consumers Trust Influencers Over Celebrities,* https://bit.ly/34Pa5HV
6. Ahmed, A., (2020, June 3), Research *Shows That YouTube Influencers Are Most Trusted by Consumers,* https://bit.ly/3z1Xa36
7. Walter, E, Gioglio, J. (2018) *The Laws of Brand Storytelling: Win—and Keep—Your Customers' Hearts and Minds,* McGraw-Hill Education; 1st edition, p. 20, P.43, P. 120, 122.
8. Mitchel, N. (2011), *Advertising & IMC: Principles and Practice* 9th Edition, P 28, https://bit.ly/3usHrGQ
9. Gilliland, N. (2021, February 18),*10 brands campaigns that took a stand on social issues,* https://bit.ly/3bTcxRv
10. Social sprout (2017), BrandsGetReal: Championing Change in the Age of social media, https://bit.ly/3wVEUqv

11. Social sprout (2018), *BrandsGetReal: What consumers want from brands in a divided society,* https://bit.ly/3fh30Gg
12. Social sprout (2017), *The Sprout Social Index: Edition XI: Social-Personality* https://bit.ly/3fcpbgB
13. Morton, J. (2019), *Why colors matters,* https://bit.ly/3fH7J2R
14. MANCINI, M. (2014, March 4) *The Real Reason Heinz EZ Squirt Ketchup Disappeared,* https://bit.ly/34c6L9k
15. Thelogocompany (2021) *Psychology of Color in Logo Design,* https://bit.ly/3yC9tTx

Chapter 16

Brand Visual Storytelling

16.1 WHAT IS A VISUAL STORY?

Visual storytelling uses images, videos, infographics, presentations, and other visuals on social media platforms to craft a graphical story around crucial brand values and offerings. A visual story is a visualization of a story containing a conflict and an escalation of events with a satisfying ending resolution. A brand must present its story that includes a solution to the customer's problem or struggle that satisfies their needs and desire. The purpose of the visual story is to convince the customer and impact their buying purchase decision to take action and enhance an emotional connection between a customer and a brand. A visual story transforms a selected set of information into a single complete static or motion picture that contains the fundamental elements of a story, designed carefully to draw the audience's attention from their starting place to the desired conclusion. For example, people dislike changing, and where possible, most people will avoid making decisions. So, the story must give them an apparent reason to act and make a change.

16.2 THE POWER OF BRAND VISUALIZATION

Marketers shall rely on visuals to amplify social media

engagement for marketing and branding purposes. (Brightcove 2018) found that 76% of consumers said they purchased a product or service after viewing a video, while 85% of millennials (18-34-year-olds) reported the same. The report proved that video is preferred for brand and marketing communication as it enhances loyalty, strengthens customer relationships, increases awareness. Further, (Brightcove 2018) research showed that people respond to visuals more intensely and quickly than text alone; 36% of consumers overall and 46% of millennials favor video content to other forms. Consumers believe it is essential to watch a video when shopping for a particular product online; personal electronics (56%), household appliances (52%), tools (48%), software (47%), clothing, and makeup (35%), and personal care (27%). [1]

    Marketers shall understand brand identity, image, values, and what it stands for as a purpose to convey it to the audience. A brand's message needs to be delivered efficiently to the customer by meeting the customer's needs, crafting the brand message into a powerful creative visual story, and communicating the brand values and culture message to the audience. Clarity and consistency are essential in visual brand storytelling to build connections with customers and grant their loyalty. When selecting footage, stock images, brand photography, and illustrations, the first step is to clarify how the visuals will represent and communicate the brand story across multiple marketing and social media channels.

16.3 SOCIAL MEDIA ROLE IN BRAND STORYTELLING

Video content is still booming. Interest in binge-watching content grew significantly during the COVID-19 pandemic, with 70% of marketers looking to up their investment in video. The competition between Instagram reels and TikTok over visual content is getting fierce. Teens (29%) preferred Instagram as a social platform of choice compared to TikTok (25%) 2. In terms of content, Instagram to continue to push story reels. Brands should consider posting short-form videos across both Instagram and TikTok rather than choosing between them.

According to a (DataReportal 2021) report, there are 4.33 billion social media users worldwide starting in 2021, equating to over 55% of the total global population. An average of two hours and 25 minutes are spent per day per person on social media. Ten billion hours spend globally using social platforms each day, which is the equivalent of nearly 1.2 million years of human existence. 3

- Facebook's active monthly users are 2.797 billion.
- YouTube's prospective advertising reach is 2.291 billion.
- Facebook Messenger exceeded 1.3 billion monthly active users.
- Instagram's reach is 1.287 billion, which provides an ideal platform for brand storytelling advertising.

Social media users are increasing each month; 9 in 10 internet users now use social media. In addition, 91% of all social media users log on to their accounts via mobile devices. These numbers justify the demand for mobile-friendly content across social media sites, which is skyrocketing. Likewise, almost 80% of the total time spent on social media sites occurs on mobile platforms (Lyfemarketing 2019). 4

   The Instagram platform is an ideal place for posting brand visual stories. An Instagram Story is a vertical slide show of images or videos. Each story lasts for 10 seconds, and the complete story reel expires after 24 hours unless users choose to highlight it on their profile. Recent Social media statistics show that the number of daily active Instagram stories users has increased from 150 million in January 2017 to 500 million in January 2019 (Statista 2019). 5 Instagram themselves reported that 500+ million people use Stories daily, and 33% of the most-viewed stories come from brands. Additionally, 87% of people said that an Instagram influencer had driven them to purchase. Instagram also revealed that 70% of "shopping enthusiasts" turn to the Instagram platform for product discovery Even if people are not buying from influencers directly, there is no denying their impact on cementing Instagram as a shopping hub.

   According to (MediaKix 2019), for those who purchase from influencers, standard image posts (78%), stories (73%), and YouTube Videos (56%) are considered the most effective types of influencer content. 6 More than ever before, people are following brands on Instagram, marking how the platform becomes rival to Facebook in terms of shopping and ads in the long run. Even if Instagram isn't stemming in direct sales, the social platform remains a vital vehicle for any social marketing funnel for educating and nurturing customers. Instagram is one of the many other social media platforms that can be used for compelling storytelling through the unique format of Instagram. Several techniques include creating one enormous picture composed of several smaller images to appeal to the reader's eyes. This technique is called Instagrids. Another excellent example is @Hershelsupply which used interesting photography displays to showcase their new products or collections:

Figure 16-1 https://www.instagram.com/herschelsupply/?hl=en

More actions can be added to Instagram stories to make them more engaging, such as adding questions, polls, and fun stickers or music to create branded content as unique as possible. Instagram stories invite brands to the possibility of higher creative freedom, which might help their campaign become a success with their audience.

Billion Dollar cited Stanford Persuasive Technology Lab (2002), which asked 2,440 participants how they evaluated the credibility of websites. Graphics has shown that website's design is the number one criterion for discerning the company's credibility according to 46.1% of people [7].In the same direction, (MDG advertising 2018) has shown that 67% of consumers consider clear, detailed images more important than product information, full description, and customer ratings in selecting and purchasing the product.[8]

HubSpot is a fantastic example of a B2B company that leverages visual content and storytelling across several social media channels. While many of the company's social media channels are showcases how B2B companies can their personality and creativity shine, encouraging engagement with influencers and prospective clients. With boards dedicated to company culture, helpful e-books, webinars, and infographics, the visual content shared is a mix of informative, humorous, and inspiring. Of course, the concept of well-composed photos is nothing new to companies—it is something they have been sourcing for their websites, advertisements, retail locations, and for the news media for a long time. What is new, though, is the concept of social media-friendly images that drive an immediate response. With professional images, techniques like retouching, food styling, set design, and lighting are commonplace. However, with social media, people are looking for images to be realistic and in line with company values and offerings.

16.3.1.1 *TripAdvisor*

In 2018, The New TripAdvisor went social into personal social-assisted travel enables members to get relevant recommendations and inspiration to become the one travel site to Plan "Your" Perfect Trip." Travelers can follow friends and travel experts they trust, including publishers, brands, and social media influencers who share information relevant to their interests. Trip Advisor allows members to post images of their hotel stays. With Millions of photos posted to the site, the value of seeing these photos is that travelers can see if the hotel truly matches the pictures shown on the hotel's website. One way to show the more human side of a brand is by putting its community's user-generated content in the spotlight.

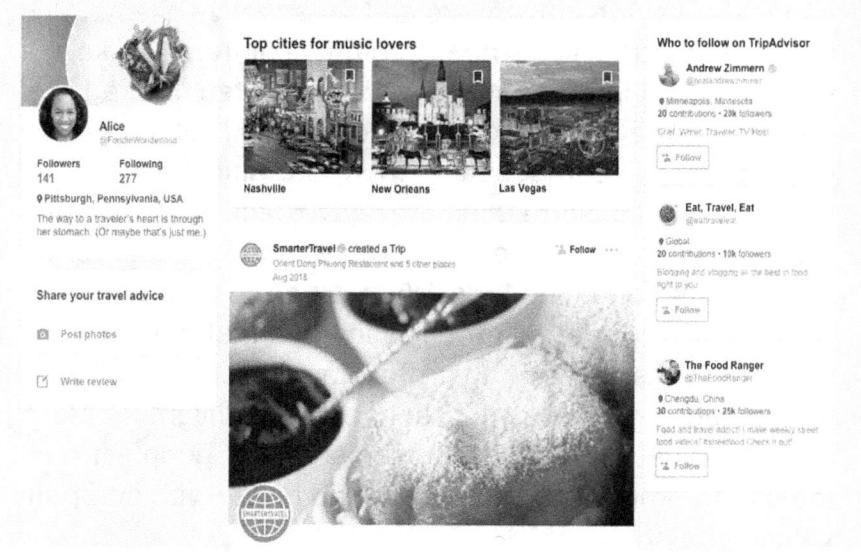

Figure 16-2 TripAdvisor aims to become social media service for travel

16.3.1.2 Lululemon, The visualization of lifestyle storytelling

A lifestyle brand is a company that will market services and products that appeal to a culture or group's interests, opinions, and attitudes. Lifestyle products will inspire and motivate people. The goal of the product is to contribute in one way or another to the consumer's lifestyle. Lululemon's primary focus is on fitness and yoga that changed the fashion industry and has been wildly successful since its founding in 1998. The success of this brand is related to the strength of its lifestyle brand and its continuous focus on product innovation. In addition, they use consistent visualization storytelling around yoga and other social-related matters in their respective digital marketing campaigns to enhance their core values among their audience and communities. For example, in one of the YouTube videos, lululemon elite ambassador Maddie Brenneman talked about her journey through life's challenges and how fly-fishing keeps her grounded https://bit.ly/3pI9TUF. Lululemon founder Chip Wilson's passion for activewear and yoga outfits led him to build an enthusiastic community around the brand movement, leading to the brand's growth. In addition, the brand sparked a sense of belonging in the customers and gets them to shop repeatedly.

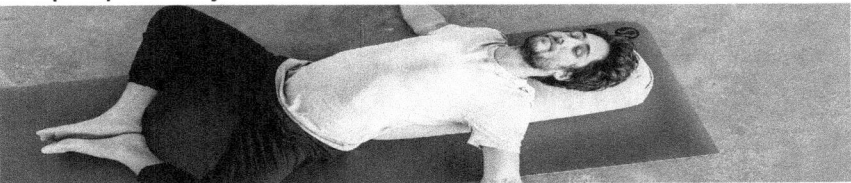

Figure16-3 Lululemon_Yoga_FathersDay_2020_Gifting_Ecomm_SlimHero

Lululemon's social media is carefully used to the best of its function: Pinterest as a catalog for its products, YouTube for easy-to-do yoga tutorial videos, and Facebook and Twitter for updates and hashtags. This is done cleverly by Lululemon by putting on classes and organizing workout groups in their active communities. The company's purpose is to be the favorite brand of those who wake up in the morning with an objective in mind, then go to bed at night with that aim completed. Lululemon ensures their customers remain connected with the brand through their social media accounts, committed to replying to as many fans as possible. The Twitter hashtag of Lululemon, which exceeds a million posts, #thesweatlife, provides a glimpse into the versatility of its products.

16.3.1.3   *Patagonia Environment Commitment*

Patagonia is one of the most influential brands and most passionate followings. Their marketing strategy, "Buy less demand more, "points to their commitment to quality, deep integrity, and cares for the environment. According to Patagonia, the clothing industry contributes up to 10% of the pollution driving the climate crisis. Today still, less than 1% of the cotton grown worldwide is organic. So, Patagonia asked employees to take cotton to 100% organic by 1996. Earlier in 2021, they asked its customers and followers to demand organic cotton https://bit.ly/357jk6y.Their visual storytelling maintains this core story of integrity and environmental stewardship. Without using supermodels, each image shows real people enjoying the outdoors, holding to cliff sides, marching through snow mountains, or throwing themselves off the sides of yachts in the

Caribbean.

Figure 16-4 Patagonia Thirty years of Patagonia

These images that communicate to a particular niche audience are the images that help the audience plan their subsequent exciting journeys.

Figure 16-5 Gear For Life Patagonia Worn Wear is Their Shop For Used Gear

Patagonia's ongoing 'Worn Wear' campaign praises the stories of the consumers that wear the company's clothes. It also keeps Patagonia gear in action longer and provides an easy way to recycle Patagonia garments beyond restoration. In addition, the company asked its customers who may have old Patagonia items to trade-in and get paid credit towards their next purchase on a used or new garment. @Wornwear is Patagonia's Instagram hub for building a loyal community around the brand values of environmental responsibility of cutting waste "Buy less, demand more." The tagline "The Stories We Wear" are profiles of professional athletes and real people who associate holes, burns, and patches with the actual scars they gather on their adventures and wear as badges of honor and accomplishment. By stitching together, the people who take pleasure in their Patagonia products and the memories they create wearing those products, the campaign tells a larger story of things worth preserving. The company wanted to prove that it produces high-quality clothes that last for years, and customers do not have to buy more, but this turns consumers more loyal to the company. It is a brave message to ask consumers not to buy more unless they need to. The tagline "Better than new" immediately show that this is no ordinary marketing effort. The "Worn Wear wagon" (pictured above) drives around the country with Patagonia to refurbish old garments and gear, sell used clothing, and hold DIY workshops https://bit.ly/3iAMiUo. Along the way, they are also reinforcing the brand's values and boosting their community of loyal fans and telling their stories in YouTube videos. In addition, they spread the word visually on social media platforms for brand followers to meet up and mend their garments.

16.3.1.4 Harvard Business Review (HBR)

The Harvard Business Review often places stories around management, professionalism, and career-life https://bit.ly/2SkjhkZ. It uses an informal tone of voice and similarly adapts long-form content into shortened Stories. However, one key difference is that HBR is a bit more interactive. While HBR embraces Instagram's poll, quiz, and other interactive Story features, it also gets creative by adding its spin on interactivity to a story. The story then gives the viewers advice on what to do if they checked any of the boxes. Readers who want to know more offer a swipe up to a long-form article on their website.

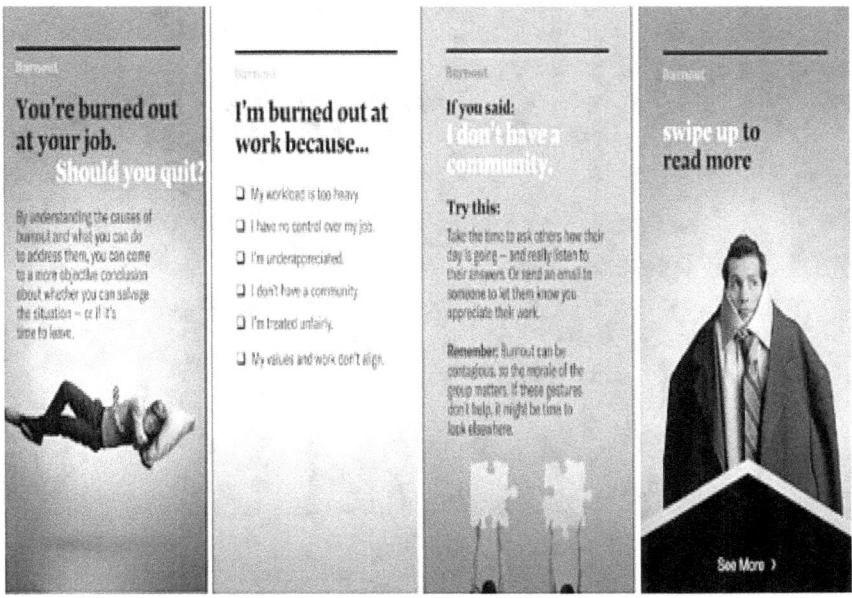

Figure 16-6
https://www.instagram.com/stories/highlights/17948277019295756/?hl=en

16.3.1.5   Moon Oral Care

Moon oral brand first launched on Instagram a series of videos to introduce their brand with a bang. It was an impactful and standout campaign for their new followers. Launching a brand on Instagram for the first time or looking to give a current feed a refresh, having a creative Instagram grid is a sure-fire way to help the brand stand out from the crowd.

Figure 16-7 https://www.instagram.com/moon/

16.4 REFERENCES

1. Georgette, K. (2018), *New research from Brightcove finds video content impacts product and service purchases, particularly by millennial consumers* https://bit.ly/3x5Bt0j
2. Barnhart, B. (2021, February 25), *The most important Instagram statistics you need to know for 2021* https://bit.ly/3cu16jG
3. Datareportal (2021, April 17) *Global social media stats* https://bit.ly/3gbjuQN
4. Sean, (2019, August 19) *32 Social Media Marketing Statistics That Will Change the Way You Think About social media* https://bit.ly/3pLn5ba
5. Tankovska, H. (2021, January 27) *Daily active users of Instagram Stories 2019,* https://bit.ly/2SuP5DF
6. Mediakix (2019), Influencer marketing 2019 industry benchmarks, https://bit.ly/2RMiAAC
7. Parkinson, M. (2016) *Do-It-Yourself Billion Dollar Graphics: 3 Fast and Easy Steps to Turn Your Text and Ideas into Persuasive Graphics, PepperLip* https://bit.ly/35fgHjc
8. Mdgadvertising (2018) *It is All About the Images [Infographic]* https://bit.ly/35eET5a

www.ingramcontent.com/pod-product-compliance
Lightning Source LLC
Chambersburg PA
CBHW060845220526
45466CB00003B/1242